FROM THE BACK OF A BUS NAMED DESIRE

From the Back of a Bus Named Desire: Essays by Brenda D. Quant

ISBN: 9781608012947

Cover design by Kevin Stone.

Printed in the United States of America.

University of New Orleans Press
2000 Lakeshore Drive
New Orleans, Lousiana 70148
unopress.org

FROM THE BACK OF A BUS NAMED DESIRE

Essays by

Brenda D. Quant

Contents

Foreword

In the early 1980s, Brenda's godson, Shawn, asked her for help with his Black History Month assignment to write about the civil rights movement of the 1960s. Brenda was a part of that movement. Little did they know that this simple request would be the genesis of the book you are reading now. At first, they just had conversations prompted by Shawn's questions, but later, Brenda would write essays for him that included her own childhood memories of segregation and how it was resisted. Soon, she began to apply her creative nonfiction writing skills to telling these stories from her life.

It is not just that she told a story; her stories emerge from the child inside wanting to be heard, felt, and understood. Brenda could tell a story from the point of view of that child, with all her emotions and youthful illusions unearthed, recollected, and brought forward:

> When I was a child, I held a deep subconscious assumption that we lived inside of the earth. This was a basic underlying fact of life that didn't need pondering any more than I would have pondered air. [. . .] One day, someone told me that we live on the outside of the world, on top of the earth, on the surface of the planet. This was the most lucid moment I had experienced up to that point in my life. Suddenly, I was unable to place myself in the cosmos. I must have had some notion of the universe because suddenly I could feel its immensity bearing down on me, and all of my awareness went instantly into fear. We had no protection, no ceiling, no roof, nothing to seal us off, seal us in. We were not curled up and cozy under a big quilt, but totally exposed. What prevented us from being hurled off the face of this whirling ball? Nothing. All of my comfort was drained away in

> an instant by this stark new reality, this rebirth trauma. I knew I would never feel safe again.

While Brenda's musings about the nature of her reality are interesting, whether inside the Earth or on its surface, her reality as a young person was filled with danger and violence that could strike a innocent child just trying to go to school at any moment. Regularly, she and her brother, Joe, had to run the gauntlet between the stone-throwing white racists and the Black nickel thieves.

Brenda could forgive the Black nickel thieves who preyed on the little children. Their purpose was to take the kids' lunch money, but the white thugs who occupied the Florida Projects a half-block from her house were different. Their purpose was cruelty. Their purpose was to hurt. In her essay "Lessons in South America," Brenda writes them off as irredeemable. Yet, as I write this, I know that Brenda knew that people, even these white racists, were capable of redemption, like St. Paul being knocked off his horse and blinded so that he could see the light. But she was not going to invest any hope in the white thugs who tormented her and her brother.

Brenda wrote that the Black thugs did redeem themselves in her view when they enforced a boycott on a store in the neighborhood that would not hire Blacks. In an interview, Brenda talked about how, at a very young age, she decided unjust laws should not be obeyed but defied and challenged. Comically, she described herself and her mother—fresh out of praying novenas at the Catholic church—as criminals. Their transgression? While the two of them waited to catch an evening bus home, her mother would act as lookout while Brenda swung in the nearby whites-only park.

Brenda's heroes were those who resisted, fought back, and found ways to punish the racists who discriminated against her and her friends. One of her stories of resistance that's not in this book is the fight Brenda and her friends waged against discrimination at the Frostop restaurant. Frostop gave white customers frosted mugs, but only paper cups to the Black customers. One day, Brenda and her friends decided to take action.

Brenda's friends who could pass for white went in and ordered the frosty drinks. Then Brenda and the darker friends came in and made a very large and expensive order, including drinks in the frosted mugs. The clerk refused to serve them the mugs, reciting Frostop's policy.

Then Brenda said, to the shock of the clerk, "You served my cousin and her friends in frosty mugs."

Now their big order was on the grill, and Brenda insisted on being served a frosted mug. When the clerk refused, everybody left.

The clerk yelled, "Wait, what about all these burgers?"

I think the response was something like, "You know where you can put them."

Brenda took the passionate desire to make a difference into adulthood, always working on the side of those being oppressed by racism, or poverty, or disability, or immigration status. All of her jobs and work addressed these injustices. When her best friend's son was born with autism, she, along with her friends, became an advocate for families with children with disabilities, eventually creating an organization to train caregivers to advocate for their children in the school system.

Through all of this, Brenda was also writing. Her articles appear in various publications. From 1996 to 1999, she served as associate editor of *Tapestry, the Journal of the Grassroots Consortium on Disabilities*. She was awarded a literature fellowship in creative nonfiction from the Louisiana Division of the Arts in 1991. Her work has appeared in *The New Orleans Tribune, Louisiana Cultural Vistas, The Other Side* magazine, *African American Review, Negative Capability Journal, THEMA Literary Quarterly, Blueprint for Social Justice, Shooting Star Review,* and other publications.

About her writing, Brenda said:

> I enjoy writing both fiction and nonfiction. However, I have become comfortable with the genre of creative nonfiction, as it lends itself to the accounting of events and experiences that are real, and ideas and concepts that may be complex, while freeing the writer to employ the techniques of fiction. Some of the elements of fiction that enliven nonfiction include developing a type of characterization through voice and tone, setting scenes through description and imagery, the use of poetic devices, verbal illustration, dialogue, dialect, and humor.
>
> Writing in the genre of creative nonfiction serves my purposes more effectively than the polemical style of traditional

> essay-writing or the fact-driven approach of journalism. I believe that it is possible to present nonfiction creatively while being faithful to truth and fact.

Yes, Brenda, it is possible to do this. Your book proves it.

— *Ted Quant*
New Orleans, May 2025

Editor's Note

Brenda Quant completed this manuscript in 2014. As with any posthumous publication, we have changed as little of her text as possible. Therefore, any temporal references in the essays refer to the time when the piece was written, not published. Also, some websites cited by Quant are no longer active. This is indicated in the bibliography section where relevant.

PART ONE

Cloak of Darkness

The New Orleans Recreation Department used to provide separate and unequal playgrounds for the city's children. Before they were desegregated in 1963 as a result of a lawsuit, there were over one hundred playgrounds for whites and only nineteen for Blacks. My family did not live near any of the Black playgrounds, and we were not allowed to set foot in Bunny Friend Park, the white playground on Desire Street, in walking distance from our house.

Holy Redeemer Church, our Black Catholic Parish (a distance of five white Catholic Churches away from our neighborhood), was across the street from Washington Square, another whites-only playground. It was a well-kept park with lots of trees, swings, a wading pool, cement paths and benches.

When I was about ten years old, Mama and I left church one Tuesday night after novena and circumnavigated Washington Square to get to the Desire bus stop at the corner of Dauphine Street and Elysian Fields Avenue. The buses were slow at night. We knew we were in for a wait. We'd been standing at the bus stop for only a few minutes when my mother suggested I break the law. There was no one around. It was dark. The large, spreading live oaks in and around the park blocked out much of the streetlight. We were standing just a few feet away from the park entrance.

"Go swing on the swings until the bus comes," Mama said.

I was the happiest criminal in New Orleans that night. I tested every swing, looking for the best fit, and thought about the little white behinds that would sit in them the next day, behinds that would never suspect that their swings had been violated during the night. I pushed off with the stealth of a cat burglar, pointed my toes at the treetops, and swung with the intensity of an Olympic athlete. I ignored the building fear of what might happen to Mama and me if we were caught.

She stood watch at the bus stop, my mother, occasionally glancing nonchalantly in my direction, but looking natural, as if she were just another colored lady waiting for a bus on a dark corner.

This was my first criminal act in life. And Mama was my co-conspirator. What happens to a child whose mother suggests, sanctions, and acts as lookout for her own daughter's crime? I became a repeat offender. A habitual swing thief. I swung on the whites-only swings every Tuesday night for the nine weeks we attended Novena that year. I was never apprehended, and I am reported to be still at large, hiding out somewhere in New Orleans.

Lessons in South America

Gravity: *First meaning: A force that acts as a bookmark on an uncertain world.*

When I was a child, I held a deep subconsciousI assumption that we lived inside of the earth. This was a basic underlying fact of life that didn't need pondering any more than I would have pondered air. The adults didn't talk about this given fact of subterranean life any more than they would remind the children to keep breathing. It was just understood. Inside this ball, we had everything we needed to sustain life. The sun and the rain clouds, the moon and stars, the animals, the growing things. Everything. God was in there with us.

One day, someone told me that we live on the outside of the world, on top of the earth, on the surface of the planet. This was the most lucid moment I had experienced up to that point in my life. Suddenly, I was unable to place myself in the cosmos. I must have had some notion of the universe because suddenly I could feel its immensity bearing down on me, and all of my awareness went instantly into fear. We had no protection, no ceiling, no roof, nothing to seal us off, seal us in. We were not curled up and cozy under a big quilt, but totally exposed. What prevented us from being hurled off the face of this whirling ball? Nothing. All of my comfort was drained away in an instant by this stark new reality, this rebirth trauma. I knew I would never feel safe again. I would have to live with uncertainty from then on. It would have to do.

Gravity*: Second meaning: Weight.*

Walking to school was dangerous for grade-schoolers on this inside-out world in the New Orleans 9th Ward. North Dorgenois Street was the shortest route to Johnson Lockett Elementary School, and there were perils along the way. We had been warned by older children to avoid a certain house on North Dorgenois Street, the house where a witch lived. I remember seeing her in her yard a few times—a middle-aged white lady in a loose-fitting cotton house dress. She cast spells on children, pinning her eyes on them and making weird hand twitches. We always crossed the street at the corner where she lived so as not to tread on the sidewalk in front of her house. Any gesture was a threat, and a sighting of the witch always made us take off running before she could turn us into frogs and spiders.

Crazy Bill was a roaming threat. He could come out of nowhere on his bicycle and chase a child down for some evil purpose. A nearly mythical figure, he was a Black teenager who could turn up anywhere in the neighborhood, his long legs pumping the pedals of his fast bicycle. Our only defense, we were told by other children, was to not speak to him or look at him, stay as far away from him as possible, and, for God's sake, don't call him Crazy Bill. That was the one thing that was sure to enrage him and cause him to chase you down. My older brother, Joe, was walking with some friends one day when there was a sudden Crazy Bill sighting. One of the boys yelled out, "Hey, Crazy Bill!", and the chase was on. The boys scattered and Crazy Bill could only pursue one of them. He chose my brother. Joe made it home intact but severely winded and angry with the friend who had yelled out.

On our trek to school, North Dorgenois Street took us the length of the all-white Florida Housing Project. Thuggish white boys, bigger than us, took delight in terrorizing Black children whose crime was walking on "their" sidewalks. For four of the seven blocks Joe and I walked to school, we negotiated the outer edge of the housing project. Once we crossed Desire Street, the color of the terrain changed, and we had to watch out for thuggish Black boys who jacked up little Black kids for their lunch money. None of them made up organized gangs—they were just random, soulless individuals.

The Black thugs, though ruthless, were less menacing than the white ones. Black thugs did not generally hurt the children they mugged. They were in it for the nickel. No child was ever offered the opportunity to vote on the matter, but given the choice, I would have preferred an assault by the Black thugs. With them, it wasn't about you personally.

You were little and defenseless and you just happened to have something they wanted: five cents. You could buy your way out of this trouble, frightening as it was.

Parallel arrangements: *Lines that run in the same direction without intersecting; they can be made of anything.*

Nature had parallels for the nickel thieves. They were predators. They stalked little ones who were far from their protective lairs. They were hardened and methodical like sharks, unmoved by the cute and fuzzy appearance of their prey. And they chose the most cowardly of all predatory ways: cannibalizing the young of their own kind.

I knew of no counterpart in nature for the white thugs. They sought nothing material. They hated us just because race hatred felt good to them, and they targeted Black children for verbal or physical assault. If they went after you, there was no way to buy your way out of trouble.

Running parallel with North Dorgenois Street was Florida Avenue, the boundary of the Florida Housing Project on the opposite side from where we lived. Florida Avenue must have been the most oddly constructed street in New Orleans. It had two sets of railroad tracks running straight up and down its middle, and parallel to the tracks was the Florida Avenue Canal. This was all bounded by two blacktopped streets that ran on each side of the avenue, all of it making up a long and ridiculous-looking avenue sandwich. Across from the Florida Project, along the other half of the sliced avenue, was the mostly Black community of single-family and double- shotgun homes. The Desire Housing Project rose up on that side of the avenue in the early 1950s to accommodate low-income Black families. The entire neighborhood, which came to be called the Desire area, could be sealed off from the rest of the city, and often was. All of the streets leading into the area were intersected by train tracks, and the neighborhood's other boundaries were canals. The endless caravans of boxcars that rumbled up and down the middle of Florida Avenue throughout the day and into the night were a moving wall that periodically shut the community off from the rest of the world.

Bridges intersected the parallel lines of the avenue connecting the two sides. The city provided a very narrow, frail wooden footbridge for pedestrians and a slightly more substantial bridge for cars. People who lived in the Desire area crossed over by the hundreds every morning. Many were school children making their way on foot to Lockett School. Many others boarded the Desire bus at the corner of Desire and Florida, "going to meet the man." They were commuters, although no one ever called them that.

The heavily trafficked intersection of Desire Street and Florida Avenue was a natural spot for the flourishing of commerce. The cluster of businesses and services included a doctor's office, a meat market with live chickens in cages on the sidewalk, a drug store, a shoe store, a grocery store, a well-baby clinic, a barber shop, the Delta Movie Theater, and a bar named Club Desire. During the day, those caged chickens squawked and complained and smelled up the area. When one chicken was chosen and removed from the cage by the butcher, all the other chickens screamed.

By day, the ever present sacrificial chickens and the clanking trains that shook the earth were a discordant background for people who waited at the bus stop, went about shopping, got prescriptions filled, took babies in for immunizations. Although the neighborhood was racially mixed, the businesses were mostly white-owned, and unless the shop's business was hair or alcohol, the managers, clerks, and cashiers were white.

There was a law against mixing Blacks and whites and alcohol under the same roof. I never knew where the white people in the neighborhood went to get drunk.

At night, the chickens disappeared from the sidewalk, the shops and offices closed, and the intersection took on the sticky smell of spilled beer and alcohol fumes as the day was put to rest with deadening spirits. Now the squawking came from people, mostly men, all of them Black, who drank inside and outside of Club Desire. They sought comfort or courage or fun from a can or a little paper bag that had shoulders. Disagreements among bar patrons sometimes led to bloodshed, or so people said. There were so many tales of violence associated with the nightlife at the corner of Desire and Florida that around the time of the Korean War, the area earned the nickname Li'l Korea.

Violence of a different kind stalked the area during daylight. School children crossing the bridge from the Desire side of the avenue at Li'l Korea were sometimes met by Black nickel thieves, posted there like scouts. "Give me your money or I'll throw you in the canal," they said to their prey. I remember many children arriving at school in tears, and nickel-less, after one of these cruel assaults. The Florida Avenue Canal was a long, deep slash in the earth. One day, I saw a car in it with just its roof showing. The pickings were easy for the thieves at that intersection with the earth-colored canal water waiting like a silent partner, ready to swallow up a fresh victim.

Who were these young Black men who preyed on Black children? Did they set alarm clocks to make sure they were at their mugging stations early enough to catch the little ones? Did they take a bath and eat breakfast before they left home?

Perpendicular angles: *Lines that can intersect parallel lines, sometimes with deadly results.*

The sense of being a target of violence was a fleshy presence that walked beside us on our way to and from school. Joe and I escaped a mugging by Black thugs, but one day a gang of white thugs targeted us. We were walking home from school bundled up in overcoats on a cold day. They spotted us—a group of white boys gathered in a long Florida Project driveway that ran perpendicular to the sidewalk. They were a distance of about half a block away from us, seven or eight greasy-haired teenagers lying in wait. I heard them before I saw them, and somehow, against all that is rational, my immediate thought was, *This is it.* I not only feared this would happen, I *knew* this would happen, and in just this way.

The boys screamed ugly names and ran at us. They cleared the project driveway and turned behind us, closing the distance between them and us with every footfall. Joe and I ran in terror, but we were blocks away from home, and I knew the long-legged boys would overtake us. They hailed rocks at us as they ran, and then one of them hurled what must have been a jagged chunk of concrete that hit Joe on the side of his face. His temple, my mother called it. Blood gushed. Once they drew blood, they called off the chase and stood on the sidewalk, yelling ugly names and threats as we kept running.

Joe had bled all over his overcoat by the time we reached home. Mama tended to his wound and checked me for damage with hands that lacked all motherly tenderness. There was a frightening, foreign thing in her touch and in her voice—a trembling rage she could not control. She was someone I couldn't recognize. I wanted to say something to comfort her, to change her back to who she'd been that morning. I wanted that person back for her sake and ours. But I couldn't speak, couldn't stop crying. And the more I cried, the more violent she became in her search for wounds on my body. My wounds weren't physical, but her hysterical search was almost like another mugging.

I knew she wanted to kill someone, anyone who lived in white skin that day. Over the next few days, her urge to commit random vengeful acts gradually subsided. I remember the accounts she gave of the incident to friends and relatives. The "thank-gods" began to show up. "Thank God the rock didn't hit him in the eye or he would have been blinded." "Thank God they were wearing thick overcoats." "Thank God his temple wasn't cut any deeper or he would have bled to death before he made it home." Terrifying blessings to be thankful for.

Geography: *A subject that should not be taught without maps.*
Discourse: *The free flow of ideas, some of which may be wrong.*

I lived to enter the fourth grade and progressed satisfactorily during that year under an affectionate, conscientious young teacher named Miss Matthews. She was pretty, petite and brown-skinned, with dark curly hair. She didn't seem to favor any child, making us feel we all had equal potential, or at least that was the effect she had on me. The city was segregated and we were not permitted to use the public library, so Miss Matthews set up a little lending library at the back of the classroom, allowing us to take books home to read. She liked to talk, but unlike other teachers I remember, she encouraged us to talk also, freeing us to ask questions and express ideas.

A few of the things I learned that year still stand out in memory. When we learned the names of the continents, Miss Matthews asked us to name the continent we lived on. We responded, like a glee club, "South America!" We knew we lived in the South. We knew we lived in America. South America was the logical answer.

"No," our teacher informed us, "we live on the continent of North America."

We were puzzled. Some of us argued the point with Miss Matthews. "We don't live in no North. We live in the South. South America." But

Miss Matthews was so insistent about her senseless version of geography that we finally had to stop arguing with her, make a great leap of faith, and swallow the illogical assertion that the South was in the North. The only alternative was to suggest that Miss Matthews could be wrong. I for one swallowed the illogical assertion, or pretended to anyway, rather than admit to the possibility that Miss Matthews was not infallible. I felt a little embarrassed for her though, as she seemed unable to grasp something even we fourth graders understood. In my heart, I knew I lived in South America. I would cling to this geographic certainty well beyond the fourth grade.

Boycott: *Not a male child; not a place to sleep.*
Carpool: *Not a type of vehicle; not a place to swim.*
Picket: *Not a fence post.*
Current events: *Subjects that, over time, become history.*

One day, Miss Matthews changed our lives. It was 1955, and she told us about a place called Montgomery, Alabama, where Negro people had stopped riding the segregated city buses. She said that they intended to continue this boycott until they received fair and equal treatment as passengers and citizens.

Boycott? What kind of mixed-up word is that, Miss Matthews?

She paced the floor at the front of the classroom, gesturing and explaining. She glowed with enthusiasm and pride, and I could feel these emotions spreading like a wave over all of us. We wanted to know more. We wanted to know how the Negroes in Montgomery were getting around town without riding the buses. "They walk, or they ride in carpools," she told us.

Carpools? The word conjured up an absurd image in my head. She explained these concepts and we got it. We kept asking questions, excited by the possibilities. The classroom buzzed. It felt as if something was released in us, some tightly constricted place that we suddenly became aware of as it began to open.

Following upon the news of Montgomery, things began to heat up all over South America. It took a few years, but the heat finally reached our neighborhood. The B&C Market was a grocery store around the corner from Li'l Korea, between the all-white Florida Housing Project, and the Black neighborhood around our school. The B&C had as many Black customers as white but did not hire Blacks for any jobs that didn't involve brooms, mops, or bicycles. A civil rights organization called the Consumers League, headed by several New Orleans ministers, addressed the unequal job opportunities for Black citizens by appealing directly to merchants.

The ministers requested a meeting with the owners of the B&C to ask that they reconsider their hiring policy in light of the fact that half of their customers were Black. The store owners refused to even meet with the community leaders, and word spread that we were to boycott the B&C until there was a change in hiring policy. Suddenly, a picket line appeared on the sidewalk outside the B&C, and even children could participate in the boycott by spending their pennies and nickels elsewhere.

Soon after the boycott began, my brother came home with a warning. "Don't go near the B&C. Some thugs on the picket line are beatin' Negroes up if they try to go in the store."

I immediately thought of the nickel thieves, imagining them moving away from their mugging stations and joining the picket line. I had just started high school at the time of the boycott, riding the bus rather than walking through the neighborhood to get to school, but I still held the childhood dread of those Black thugs. None of them had ever attacked us, but they had been a daily source of fear. Because of them, we had to walk from our racially mixed neighborhood, where we were called names routinely, through an all-white area in which we could be assaulted and battered and could possibly bleed to death or be blinded by rock-throwing white thugs, cross dangerously busy Desire Street without benefit of stop sign, traffic light, or crossing guard to get to the relative safety of a Black school in a Black neighborhood, and then come face to face with a crying kindergartner who has just been robbed under the threat of being flung into the Florida Avenue Canal—by someone Black!

That there were such people on the planet had confused and frightened me. I needed to somehow redeem them, see them bring their talent for violence and intimidation to the picket line.

Redemption: *Forgiving oneself and others, but not all others.*

The white thugs were beyond redemption, forever cut off by their wall of hate.

Crazy Bill did not need redemption. He was never really a superhuman terrorist on a bicycle. He was a drugstore delivery boy who suffered from epileptic seizures. I have an early memory of a tall, slim boy who had a seizure just outside our front door. My mother went to his aid and sat on the steps with him until he was able to stand on his own. On the day that my brother was chased by Crazy Bill, my mother made me realize that he was the same boy she had so tenderly nursed back to consciousness a few years before. She said it was a terrible thing to ridicule people for having seizures. Before that moment, I had not understood that Crazy Bill was the same boy I had seen in such a vulnerable state, and in an instant, Bill went from menace to victim in my eyes. He was not crazy or dangerous; he was a target of prejudice. He wasn't Crazy Bill, he was Bill. The real terrorists were the children who taunted him. They were the ones in need of redemption. Bill was just a boy with a job—a job that had brought him to our doorstep with a drugstore delivery on that day when he collapsed in convulsions.

The white witch did not need redemption, either. She was deaf. And those hand gestures that so terrified us? American Sign Language. Learning this caused me some shame. When we had seen her moving her hands, she might have been trying to say hello to us, or she could have been just scratching her nose. But in our ignorance, we always ran from her.

I held out hope for the Black thugs, visualizing them on the picket line. But well after the B&C boycott, I learned that there were no thugs on the picket line, no threats of beatings or canal flingings. The rumors of violence were just that: rumors. The Consumers League had trained its forces in nonviolence. They did not even tolerate threats of violence. Yet in the end, even though there were no thugs on the picket line, a violent act played a major role in the outcome of the B&C boycott. The picketers, mostly college students from various parts of the city, were taunted by white onlookers, and when a white man yelled "nigger," one of the picketers became enraged, lost sight of the goal, and attacked the name-caller. This action gave the B&C owners the legal grounds they needed to banish the picket line. People remained free to boycott the store, but the power of organization and visibility was lost. Time went by, people either observed the boycott or chose not to. The Consumers League went on to lead successful actions in other neighborhoods of the city, and eventually the B&C owners sold the store and left the neighborhood. But South America would never be the same.

The concept of nonviolence entered our awareness, and I came to understand the wisdom of that message. Over the years, new activist groups appeared in the neighborhood. One group adopted the poetic name Sons of Desire. And there was another group that I had sort of wished into existence called The Thugs United, Inc.: redeemed thugs steering young men away from crime.

* * *

It turned out that Miss Matthews was right about New Orleans being on the North American continent. My brother's godmother gave him a globe for his birthday one year—the world rendered small enough to occupy space on his dresser. The colorful cardboard sphere could spin on its axis, a feature that invited us to treat the object like a toy. We made up a game. The one who was "it" had to point to the spinning globe and pronounce the name of the place they were pointing to when the world stopped turning.

And then what? Beyond the spinning and pointing, I can't remember what the object of our game was, or what constituted a win. But being able to touch the world with my fingers led to my eventual relocation to North America.

The Resistance

When the bus was crowded, the white faces surrounding me in the front were an obstacle course as I boarded. I had to squeeze through them, denying that any interracial touching was happening, and take my stand in the rear. We could all do this mental trick, us coloreds and whites who rode the buses and streetcars during segregation. We could touch each other, inhale each other's coffee-and-chicory, grits-and-egg, cornflakes-and-milk breath, fall into each other on the pitching bus, compelled by the legal requirement that we occupy our assigned turf and, once there, deny everything.

The "screen" separated New Orleans bus and streetcar passengers by race. Blacks rode in the back, whites in front. From the rear, I had a perfect view of that length of wood called the screen. I grew up in its shadow from babygirlhood into adolescence. Its name did not suit it at all. It was a rectangular piece of wood, a short plank about an inch thick, a foot or so long, and about three inches high. One side read "*FOR COLORED PATRONS ONLY*"; the other side read "*FOR WHITE PATRONS ONLY.*" The screens were varnished to a high gloss, their black lettering done in even, bold strokes. The wood had two metal pegs drilled into the bottom edge, allowing them to be placed upright and snug on any seat-back rail—a metal tube with two holes to accommodate the screen's pegs.

My father was a carpenter. He could cradle a piece of wood in his hands, apply imagination and power tools, and coax the innocent cypress or oak or cedar into a thing of utility and beauty. The wood had no intent of its own—it had to comply with the designs of its master. Some anonymous bus company craftsmen employed their skills to create hundreds of those fine, sturdy chunks of wood, the edges of which were softly rounded from decades of handling. They looked as permanent as a valued antique. The finished product was an assault to the eyes and the spirit.

The biracial "*COLORED/WHITE*" sign was a moveable evil. If you were a Black passenger and there were empty seats behind you, you were expected to move farther back, taking the screen with you, filling all seats behind it and leaving any empty seats in front of it for the convenience of white passengers. Black passengers could also move the screen forward when the back of the bus filled up and there were available seats in the front. If you were white, and the closest empty seat to the front of the bus was behind the screen, you simply moved it back and took your seat in front of it.

But there was no rule that said that a white bus rider had to move the screen for the convenience of Black passengers, and this could lead to racially tinged pranks. Aunt Phil told me that in the 1930s and '40s, it often happened that a white person would move the screen all the way to the back of the streetcar, even though there might have been only a few white passengers and a throng of Black ones. This instantly turned all but the last seat into the white section. Black passengers then had to give up their seats and stand bunched up in the rear while the streetcar rolled and swayed along, empty from the rear forward. I asked Aunt Phil if people tried to get the conductor to do something.

"Sure," she said, "people complained, but I never saw a conductor do anything about it."

* * *

I'd always thought the word "screen" was an odd name for that length of wood, but years after it vanished, I learned that up until the early part of the twentieth century, when public transit consisted solely of streetcars, an actual screen—a large rectangle of wire mesh—divided the cars in half for the purpose of racial separation. Prior to the days of the metal screen, there were separate streetcars for Blacks and whites, with the Black cars marked with a star. Only a few cars on each line were designated as star cars, and while whites were free to ride on any car and sit anywhere, Blacks had to wait on a star car for their rides. And some streetcar lines did not allow Black passengers to ride at all.

Unlike their wooden stand-in, the metal screens were fixed permanently to one spot, creating rear compartments on each side of the aisle. When buses replaced some of the streetcars, the screen became imaginary and moveable, a piece of wood to holding its place. It was up to the weighty task of separating humans, yet it was light enough for a small child to lift easily. A white child of four could tippy-toe and stretch and reach it to impose the barrier and banish us all behind it. Such power! A Black child had the equal opportunity to move the screen about in an act of forced cooperation with the dehumanizing practice. Children on both sides of the screen absorbed some of life's lessons this way: fitting pegs into holes, learning shapes and relationships, geometry and sociology, woodcraft, penmanship, and civics, all in one easy, repetitive lesson.

* * *

Sometimes the screen wasn't there at all, yet the imaginary line had to be held.

In the early 1950s, Uncle Joseph and Aunt Juanita moved their family to Delery Street in the Lower 9th Ward. Their neighborhood was a distance away from any city bus line, so a small business sprang up to fill a need, running a bus line in the isolated, majority Black neighborhoods of the 9th Ward. The line consisted of a few rickety old school buses painted blue, and while the city buses charged seven cents, the blue bus charged a nickel. Passengers christened it The Nickel Bus.

I was seven or eight years old the first time I rode The Nickel Bus. I was with Aunt Juanita, and we were headed to her house on the last street in the city. She paid our fares and walked to the back. I stood at the front of the bus for a moment looking for the screen and soon realized that there wasn't one, and there were no white passengers on the bus either. Liberation! I plopped down in the front seat. When Aunt Juanita reached the back of the bus and turned to see me sitting just behind the driver, she nearly panicked.

"Brenda Ann, come here. You can't sit up there."

I moved to the back and sat next to her, obedient and embarrassed. But I protested. "There's no screen, Aunt Juanita. Why do we have to sit in the back when there's no screen and no white people either?"

Some of the passengers laughed quietly. Some shook their heads. Was their judgment meant for me or for Aunt Juanita or for the stoic white man driving the bus? I couldn't tell. It didn't occur to me then that they could have been shaking their heads at the whole ridiculous system. I can't remember what Aunt Juanita said to me after that, except that she provided some fuzzy words of explanation that made me realize I didn't have a good grasp of the lesson of the screen, that even without the "normal" set up, we were expected to screen ourselves, to police our own fannies and pretend there was a screen when even a child could see that it did not exist.

Segregation etiquette for city buses was formalized, with edicts from high places. A 1928 memorandum from the superintendent of transportation remained in force until the desegregation of public transportation. It instructed operators not to use force but to "call the first Police Officer you meet and enlist his aid" in dealing with a noncompliant "colored passenger."[1]

My mother was sitting just behind the wooden screen on the St. Charles streetcar one day in the early 1940s. Some Black people who were sitting behind her got off the streetcar, leaving empty seats behind the screen and right behind her. Mama was expected to move herself and the screen farther back so that all empty seats would be in front of the screen, in the white section.

She did not comply with that expectation.

"I was holding an armload of packages, and didn't bother to get up just to move a few seats back," she told me. "My stop was coming up soon anyway, and besides, there were still some empty seats in front of the screen."

But the conductor was conscientious in his role as enforcer. He stopped the streetcar, got out of his seat, and walked the distance to where Mama sat. He stood over her and ordered her to move back. She refused. He threatened to call the police.

"Call 'em," she said.

He then yanked the screen from the seat in front of her and slammed it into the railing of the seat behind her. Metal clanged against metal, like the sound of a cell door closing. The seat where Mama sat was instantly transformed into the forbidden whites-only section. There she was, sitting in front of the screen, a criminal, subject to arrest and prosecution and god-knows what else.

"*JesusMaryandJoseph*, Mama!" I gasped. "What happened?"

"I told the man I didn't care if he threw the screen out the window, I wasn't gettin' up until my stop came!"

"What did he do then?"

"He went back to his little conductor seat and drove the streetcar."

When my friend Jerome was a little boy riding the bus by himself one day, he took the screen from a seatback rail and threw it on the floor. He had seen his father once do the same thing. The driver was about to call the police.

"I was scared, I was crying," Jerome says, "and then this old woman, an old Black woman I didn't even know, told the driver and some of the white passengers, 'Please don't call the police. I'm going to take this boy home and see that his grandmother bust his behind. This boy gives too much trouble.'" The driver let the old woman take Jerome off the bus, and she led him behind a store as the bus pulled off. "The old lady grabbed me and hugged me and kissed me and told me she was proud of me."

On his seventeenth birthday, my friend Cecil and his college friends, a group of young men and women, were returning from a basketball game on a city bus in 1954. The screen mysteriously vanished. One of them had thrown the offending piece of wood out of a window. Some whites boarded the bus, and with no screen, they did not know where to sit. The bus did not move. It was as if the vehicle had lost a vital mechanical part and was incapacitated. The driver demanded that someone produce the screen or tell him what had happened to the critical race separator, but the students only laughed and refused to give up any information. The driver called the police.

Cecil remembers: "They said, 'If the screen doesn't reappear, we're gonna take all of you to jail.' We said, 'OK, that's what you're gonna have to do.'" All of them were arrested.[2]

* * *

When you have to be someplace at an appointed hour every morning, you internalize the equation "distance equals speed times time." You hustle. I made a major life change in the sixth grade, going from public to Catholic school, from a long walk to a long bus ride. I had to factor the schedule of the Desire bus into my new academic life and save myself, my parents, and all of my ancestors from the stigma of tardiness.

Others hustled to get to their destinations: adults motivated by paychecks, students motivated by the need for education or by the fear of not having one. All of these strangers converged each morning on the buses.

The Desire bus route was as familiar as family to me. I'd ridden the line so regularly and for so many years that my whole being knew every stop, every turn. There were several Catholic churches along the route, and as was the custom of the time, people made the sign of the cross each time the bus went past one of the churches, acknowledging a fleeting common bond. The bus company provided a free weekly newsletter called *The Rider's Digest,* a pamphlet-sized foldout filled with local news, recipes, homemaking tips, and jokes. Passengers alternated between reading *The Rider's Digest* and fanning themselves with it on the sticky, hot bus. The brakes squealed at every stop, the metal pegs of the screens rattled on their seatback rails, the hot exhaust that spewed from the underside radiated into the interior and was always more intense at the rear. Often, teenaged boys gathered on that long seat at the back of the bus. It was the worst seat in the house, but they not only owned that space, they celebrated it by singing Mardi Gras Indian songs and chants. This is how I learned "Jock-a-mo-fee-no-ah-nah-nay," "Iko-Iko," and "Two Way Pak E Way."

Over the many years that I was a daily rider, faces of strangers became familiar, even though the people belonging to those faces mostly remained strangers. Sometimes I even knew which faces to expect to see boarding and getting off at certain stops. There was one face in particular that I was always interested to see, a young white woman who boarded the bus some mornings. She usually sat on the long seat behind the driver, and if there were no seats, someone usually got up to offer her theirs. Her hair was mouse-colored and always looked pinched and starched and immobile. She wore prim-looking skirts and blouses and a little too much make-up. She was nondescript and would have been nearly invisible were it not for her deformity: a severely hunched back that completely doubled her over. She was a walking right angle, straining to appear unburdened while carrying this heavy burden on her back and struggling to look where she was going.

She was either an old teenager or a young adult, and I couldn't help wondering about her life—her desires, dreams, and limitations. Could she dance? Did she have girlfriends? Would she ever have a boyfriend? She had no school books in her arms, so I wondered if she was headed to a job.

Everyone stared at her. It showed on her face that she would never become accustomed to the stares. I admired her for venturing out, riding the bus to wherever it was she was headed, the starers be damned. There was something motivating about seeing her face the world with a confidence that I knew she must have struggled to build. I heaped pity on this girl for years from my side of the screen and concentrated on not staring at her.

New Orleans public transportation was desegregated in 1958 as a result of a lawsuit and federal court order. The bus and streetcar drivers piled up the obsolete screens in a clearing on company property and set them on fire. I learned this from an elderly man who had been a streetcar conductor back then, when all of the drivers and conductors were white. He said that the operators had grown sick of being the race screen enforcers and were happy to see all that wood go up in flames. But while that fire blazed, a cross was burning in uptown New Orleans on the front lawn of the federal judge who signed the public transit desegregation order.

* * *

I started high school just after public transit desegregation, and remained a daily Desire bus passenger. The screens had vanished. Craftsmen were again called upon, but this time their job was to fill in the holes that held up the wooden screens on the seatback rails for so many decades. Now we could sit anywhere, even on the long sideways seats in the very front of the bus, just behind the driver. The screen had never reached the extreme front of the bus, and those two long seats had always been off limits. So it became a common sight to see a nearly empty bus with ten Black people bunched together on the two long seats in front. We were testing out an experience we'd been denied: riding sideways.

Riding in front was more than a novelty. Most white passengers were slow to accept Negroes sitting all over the place. They held onto their old ways by refusing to sit behind us, choosing to stand, even if it meant standing behind us, rather than lower themselves into a seat behind where the screen would have been. If they were already sitting when a Negro sat in front of them and there were no available seats in front of the offending Negro, they stood. And of course, if a Negro sat next to a white person, the white person almost invariably shot up as if the seat had suddenly been electrified.

This situation led to devilment. If a few Blacks sat in the long seats in the very front of the bus, it meant that the entire bus was behind the non-existent screen and off limits to whites. We took advantage of this peculiarity and clustered up front at every opportunity. We also took up as many seats as we could, sitting all over the bus in singles rather than in pairs. Even best friends would split up and sit in different seats. The unspoken strategy was to make them choose between sitting behind us, or sitting next to us, or standing all the way to their destinations. For months they chose the vertical option.

There was some ugly retaliation. Some whites got physical, pushing Black passengers to the floor of the bus. But after some time passed, most of the white passengers began to rationalize that sitting behind us was tolerable. Sitting next to us was still months away for the majority of white passengers, years for some.

One morning, during the public transit reconstruction period, I boarded the bus and sat on the long seat in front. I was still a front-seat junkie then. I must have been late that morning because the bus was not crowded. The young white woman with the hunched back who so fascinated me was sitting on the other end of the same seat, leaving a big space between us. As soon as my behind touched the seat, hers was up. She moved with speed that I did not think her capable of, grabbing the vertical bar and swinging her bent body to the other side of the bus, to the other long seat, where some white people were sitting. She landed there recklessly, her face flushed with indignation.

The other white people glared at me. The fact that I was the target of a dramatic insult did not register with them. To them, I was the offender. I had endangered this fragile creature—made her leap up so fast that she could have fallen over. *Why prey on the weakest person on the bus?* their eyes asked. *Have you no shame?*

I had no shame. Only anger. I stared at the girl until I got off the bus. I gloated over her hump and my lack of one. I thought how like a ridiculous animal she looked, swinging herself across the bus in that comic posture. Most of all, I cursed myself for having squandered years of sympathy and admiration on this unworthy person.

I remember these thoughts clearly because it was frightening to me that I could have such thoughts. But I was powerless to stop the thoughts and the staring. I'd been sitting down next to white people on the bus for months, expecting them to leap up. Usually they did. It had become a quest—seeing how many of them I could propel per week. But I had not expected this young woman to be among the leaping whites.

During all those years that I'd lavished concern and sympathy on her, I had built up a sense of superiority. I thought that despite segregation, poverty, and unequal opportunity, I had a better life than she did. I could stand up straight. I could dance. I was going to have a boyfriend someday. I thought that "white-skin privilege" was wasted on her, that if she could have chosen whether to be born with a bent white body or a straight Black one, she would have chosen to be Black. Who wouldn't? And so, from my position of straight-backed superiority, I had shown this girl some kindness, if only in my head.

But the moment she sprang up and spun away from me, I knew I was wrong about her. I felt that when she looked at me, she must have thought, *I may be bent up, but at least I'm not a nigger, and I don't have to sit next to one.*

Segregation brought out the ugliest of emotions on both sides of the screen.

* * *

Catholic schools were desegregated in 1962, when I was starting twelfth grade. By then, the vanishing of the screen was four years behind us, and people had gotten over it for the most part. The archdiocese sponsored several programs that fostered interaction among Black and white Catholic school students. One such event was a day-long student conference at a monastery on the north shore of Lake Pontchartrain, and our school principal selected my best friend Ursula and me to attend and participate.

Ursula's dad sacrificed his only day off from work to drive us to the monastery early on that Sunday morning across the twenty-six-mile causeway that spans the lake. We would be returning that afternoon on a Greyhound bus, and he would meet us at the station. En route to the monastery, miles ticked by under the tires of Daddy Arceneaux's old family-sized sedan.

I can't remember the conference topic or any details about it, only that Ursula and I did a good enough job and managed to get out of there without embarrassing our school or our people. We looked forward to our bus ride back to New Orleans.

We boarded in the Northshore town of Covington and sat up front. A few other people got on, leaving the bus about three-quarters empty. The bus lingered even after everyone was settled in. There was a quiet commotion among the passengers, and the driver got off the bus a few times. Something was up. I noticed that an elderly white woman was standing just inside the door of the bus, right next to the driver's seat. A passenger sitting across from us offered her their seat. I never heard the woman speak a word, but she made it clear in the way she turned away from that person that she was refusing the offer.

The driver spoke directly to the woman, but I couldn't hear what he said. Then he got the bus in gear and set out with the elderly woman standing up front, holding on. Ursula and I exchanged looks and hushed words as it dawned on us that, by standing, the woman was making a statement that involved us. We were the only Black passengers on the bus. Had she taken the seat offered to her, she would have been sitting directly across from Ursula and me, and all other available seats were behind us.

"Is she really going to stand up all the way to New Orleans?" I whispered. "Naw, she'll get tired of this once we get to the Causeway," Ursula answered.

But she never did sit down. Her racial nostalgia kept her a stagnant relic of the past. She stood all the way across the twenty-six-mile bridge, and she seemed to have the sympathy of everyone on the bus except us. No one asked us to move to the rear, but looking around at the other passengers, our gazes were met with what I assumed to be their condemnation. *How can you be so cruel as to make this old lady stand up on a moving bus?* I felt this question hanging in the air. Our response was to be as visibly cheerful as possible, and that wasn't difficult. We were already jubilant that our conference participation had gone well, we were two best friends together on an outing, we were world travelers speeding toward home with stories to tell, and we did our best to ignore the white-haired lady standing just feet away. The more the white passengers stared daggers into our backs, the more furiously gleeful our chatter became.

I was not entirely oblivious to the woman's suffering. I was raised to respect my elders, and one of the most common ways to show respect was to give up my seat on the bus to an old person, something I was always proud to do. The same courtesy applied to anyone with a disability. But here I was in a position where one value faced off against another equally strong value. Respect my elder, or preserve my own dignity. Should I voluntarily move to the rear?

Should I grant this woman the right to demean me for the sake of her own racial comfort?

Today, I have a retroactive sense of compassion for that lady when I picture her. She endured a long, uncomfortable ride, and that was unfortunate. But the saddest part of her ordeal had nothing to do with me. Four years after the bonfire that marked the disappearance of the screen, she remained trapped by it, hostage to some notion of racial superiority. That day, as she chose to stand and hold on to a railing on the moving bus, I chose to hold on to all of the dignity I had earned in my young life.

Running While Black

The Desire bus route, having no beginning or end of the line, meanders restlessly curling and looping as it snakes its outbound way through the 9th Ward via Desire Street, cuts between the Florida and the Desire Housing Projects, and turns upriver, slipping through the Bywater, the Marigny, and the French Quarter as it winds its inbound way to Canal Street—the functional, if not the geographic, center of town. Then it snakes back and descends downriver, downtown, resuming its outbound course.

The Galvez bus route is much more predictable and straightforward. It runs up Miro and down Galvez—two parallel streets a block apart—with little deviation and having a beginning and end of the line. It's a straight arrow that pierces the looping Desire route at two points eight blocks apart.

The Desire bus that Paul targeted that night crossed Galvez Street, made its big loop around the Florida Housing Project, and turned onto Mazant Street headed toward the Mississippi River. Several blocks into Mazant Street, its route would intersect again with Galvez Street. Paul knew this. He knew the two routes as well as the drivers did. He also knew that the shortest distance between two points is a straight line. So while the Desire bus driver was compelled to follow a big arc of a path to get to the intersection of Mazant and Galvez, Paul could take Galvez Street, a straight arrow of eight blocks. If he ran fast enough, he could meet the bus there and deliver a message to the white driver who had just intentionally pulled off and left him. Paul, a brown-skinned, lean, swift-footed teen, carried humiliation and rage for all of the left-behind Black citizens, and he carried a big brick he'd picked up along the way. Paul got there just as the bus rolled up to the intersection. It was a direct hit. He threw his brick with such force that the entire windshield of the bus shattered. He ran home, savoring the vengeance.

* * *

Up until 1961, all of the New Orleans bus and streetcar drivers were white at a time when about a third of the population was Black. Many of the drivers seemed to live for the opportunity to leave Black would-be passengers on the sidewalk in a choking cloud of exhaust. Running while Black provided the drivers with a perfect opportunity to inflict abuse. You could be umbrellaless in a downpour with an armload of school books, you could be pulling a child by the hand, you could be old and arthritic—no matter. If you were Black, you were always at risk of petty victimization by a sadistic white driver.

It happened all over town. Black passengers already on a bus with a driver who had committed such an offense would register empathy for the left behind—shaking heads, sighing, sucking teeth, and whispering curses at seeing their brethren humiliated and inconvenienced.

It happened in cities across the South. In Montgomery, Alabama, Black passengers had to board and pay their fares at the front of the bus, climb off, and re-board through the back door.

This gave white drivers the chance to drive off without you after you had paid your fare. This was one of the bitter complaints lodged by the Black patrons who launched the 1955 Montgomery bus boycott that changed the course of American history.

* * *

Paul, his parents, and five siblings lived in our block, and he was like an older brother to me. He often roamed the city after school and on weekends and relied on the labyrinth of bus routes to get him home at all hours. Recounting his travels, he'd call exotic names of Uptown streets and bus lines that were outside my realm of experience. Paul had a girlfriend, a bicycle, and a newspaper route. He loved jazz and tried to impose it on the rest of us. His younger sister, Ev, said it sounded like a band tuning up. I had to agree. His worst habit was putting mayonnaise on his hot dogs. Weiner steam caused the mayonnaise to liquefy and separate and run. Disgusting. One year, he was cast in the role of Ebenezer Scrooge in the Lockett School Christmas play. My brother played the Ghost of Christmas Past. The two of them rehearsed lines at our house.

On the night of the shattered windshield, Paul had probed the secrets of the dark city sufficiently for one night and was on his way home. It was late. Few buses were running. He got off a Galvez bus intending to transfer to a Desire. Fortune smiled, and a Desire bus, all lit up from the inside like a beacon against the night, empty except for its driver, pulled up just as Paul hopped off the Galvez bus. The driver saw him running across the street with a paper transfer in hand. Fortune smiled on the driver, too, presenting him with one more opportunity to debase one more Black person that night. The driver waited at the stop in his empty bus, waited until the young man had safely crossed the street, waited with his door open, and just as Paul was about to lift a foot to board the bus, the driver pulled the handle that slammed the door in his face.

I can only imagine the curses Paul heaped on the driver, the driver's mother, the driver's whole race. But it wasn't enough. Curses are unreliable. Only direct action would satisfy Paul on that night, and the abuse was avenged.

A few days after his act of retaliation, Paul told me what he had done. I would have been about thirteen then, and Paul sixteen. I was stunned by the violence and lawlessness of his act. The nonviolent movement for racial justice had already been widely embraced as the wisest way forward throughout the South. This wasn't it.

Paul went on talking about the physics of his vengeful act, marveling at the fact that the brick had completely taken out that huge windshield. He had thought the impact would startle the driver and bounce off the thick glass, leaving only cracks. He had not anticipated the spectacular results he'd achieved. Meanwhile, I was transforming right in front of him. I was suddenly impressed by the audacity, the bold directness of his deed. The nonviolent strategies—the boycotts, picket lines, petitions, lawsuits, marches—would yield results someday, but Paul's method was so immediately satisfying that I was seduced by its aggressive precision. I visualized him running through the dark street. I thought of all the times it had happened to me, times I'd seen it happen to Black people at bus stops all over. Paul could have been dressed in the chain mail of a knight, gripping a pointed javelin in his hand instead of a brick, astride a magnificent steed galloping through the 9th Ward on his way to slay a dragon at Galvez and Mazant, and he would not have looked any more heroic to me than he suddenly did at that moment.

I hoped that the driver of that Desire bus knew that the young Black man who hurled that brick was the same person he had debased moments before, that he saw him running up to the bus with a brick instead of a bus transfer. But on that dark corner, the driver probably did not see much, and that was fine. The act was about more than this one driver and this one Black patron. It was a momentary balancing of the scales for all of us. It felt good.

The movement for rights and dignity maintained its nonviolent character overall, Paul's exploits notwithstanding. In 1961, when I was in high school and still a regular bus patron, the bus company hired its first Black drivers. Paul's brother, Archie, was hired as a bus driver, and this was a source of family and neighborhood pride. I saw many white patrons refuse to board buses driven by Black men, but eventually Black drivers were a common sight, and reluctant whites gave in and got on the damned bus.

Time passed. More racial barriers came down. I became a student at the University of New Orleans in 1963. One morning, as I was standing at the bus stop at Elysian Fields Avenue and Miro Street, I saw a Black garbage man for the first time in my life. We were moving up.

PART TWO

Desire Lines

A desire line is an earthen path etched by repeated footfalls. It is an improvised course that is the most direct means of getting from one point to another.[3] In the absence of a constructed pathway, humans make a way. Paved paths are planned; desire lines just happen. Viewed from above, well-worn desire lines look like narrow erasures on the green landscape. When a trailblazer ignores a sidewalk to assert a more direct route, the resulting trampled grass becomes a strip of packed, bare earth as others are drawn to the most efficient way to reach a destination.

Desire lines can be ancestral. "Many streets in old cities began as desire lines which evolved over the decades or centuries."[4] Ancient paths also ramble through our history in symbolic ways, traversing land and sea.

* * *

Jesus brought the first Africans to the thirteen colonies as cargo. *Jesus* was a German-built ship purchased by the British king Henry VIII for his navy, then inherited by Queen Elizabeth I, who partnered with a slaver who pirated a Portuguese ship at sea, stole its captive Angolans, and sold them in Jamestown, Virginia. The year was 1619, twelve years after the founding of Jamestown, the oldest settlement in the colonies. British blue bloods established the Royal Adventurers Company, and the plundering of the African continent brought such great wealth to the queen that she knighted *Jesus*'s captain and rewarded him with a coat of arms depicting a captive African bound with rope.[5]

Desire was the first American-built slave ship. She was constructed and armed in Marblehead, Massachusetts, her belly outfitted with leg irons, bars, and racks. In 1637, a year after the founding of Harvard University, seventeen years after the landing of the Pilgrims at Plymouth

Rock, *Desire* set sail for the British West Indies and returned seven months later with cotton, tobacco, and enslaved Africans who'd labored on Caribbean plantations. The Africans were quickly bought up by enterprising Massachusetts citizens.[6]

A philosopher writes, "In reality, history is the history of desire."[7] A historian writes that naming their first slave ship *Desire* was "symbolic of New England's desire to make money as transporters of slaves into the various North American and Caribbean colonies."[8] Other slave ships carried equally revealing names, such as *Royal Fortune* and *Treasurer.* Some investors paved over their material objectives, crisscrossing sea lanes in ships that bore hallowed names like *Grace of God, Angel,* and *Lord.*[9]

* * *

Desire lines are simultaneously creative and destructive. Conservationists warn that desire lines, also known as social trails, can be detrimental to ecology and habitat, causing erosion and scarring of the landscape.[10]

Desire did not make its maiden voyage with an empty belly. She sailed from New England to the West Indies laden with dried fish, Boston rum, and Pequot Indians. The Massachusetts and Connecticut militias slaughtered great numbers of Pequots. Of those who survived, many of the women and children were enslaved in New England, but some of them were transported to the British West Indies as slaves.[11] Thus it was Native Americans rather than Africans who were the first cargo on the first American-built slave ship. A trail was blazed. *Desire* went on to make many more human-swapping voyages, altering the landscape with every crossing.

Soon after *Desire*'s first voyage, Massachusetts etched slavery into its legal code—the Body of Liberties.[12] Rhode Island's founder, Roger Williams, who also established the first Baptist Church in the colonies, referred to the Pequots as "Adam's degenerate seed."[13] The New Englanders declared the Pequots extinct, banned their language, and even forbade the speaking aloud of the name Pequot.[14] As the numbers of Native Americans declined, the population of Africans in the New World soared. The path to wealth and devastation between Africa and the embryonic nation of America came to be called the Middle Passage.

* * *

The act of creating a desire line is sometimes called wayfinding.[15]

New Orleans, where I live, boasts of a historic 9th Ward street named Desire. Some of our wayfinding historians romanticize the covetous name, Frenchifying it, beating a watery route over oceans to link the name to the Old World. Lovelorn lore claimed that Napoleon Bonaparte pursued a woman called Desiree Clary who rejected him and married the future king of Sweden. The name Desiree means "much desired"[16]—the perfect complement for a compelling love story.

In reality, Desire Street was named for a different woman. It was carved out of an antebellum plantation in the nineteenth century, plowing its way through the large landholding of a wealthy New Orleans man. He named the street after his daughter, Desiree de Montreuil, who was born in 1790.[17]

* * *

My family history is fragmented, but I know that some of my ancestors arrived on this continent by slave ship. Half a century after the Civil War, my grandfather, John Guillory Sr., purchased farmland on a rural road in Opelousas, Louisiana. A former sharecropper, he went on to earn a living growing cotton for market, raising subsistence crops and livestock for his family, and working at a sawmill. Other Guillorys lived on the same road, and in the 1990s, when the city proposed that the roads be given names to replace their prosaic Parish numbers, my uncle, John Guillory Jr., suggested Guillory Road.

To his great disappointment, the city fathers and mothers were not persuaded. A Guillory Road, they explained, already existed outside Opelousas but within the Parish boundaries. Apparently, it is possible to have too many Guillorys. The officials soon decided on Desiree Road as the new name, presumably honoring yet another much desired woman.

* * *

Architects, landscapers, and city planners study desire lines in order to incorporate them into new designs. A traffic engineer is quoted as saying that desire lines "indicate yearning."[18]

Learning the name of this age-old phenomenon has brought anonymous people who walked before me into my awareness. I happened upon a path recently when I accompanied a young relative on a mission. My fifth cousin Katie, a high schooler, had to report to New Orleans Juvenile Court for truancy. The most direct route to the court section was not the bank of plate glass doors that front the government building, but a small entrance at the end of a path that cut across a wide lawn. Within a few footfalls on that path, I realized that I was traversing a desire line, striding across history, albeit on a very small scale. Though the trail was covered with gray cement pavers, I was certain it had begun its life as a desire line. The lawn that it bisected was squared off by professionally poured sidewalks. Clearly, this snaky line of pavers, this three- foot-wide afterthought, disguised an earthen path that was born of the yearnings of multitudes of juveniles summoned to court over the years. Apparently, someone had decreed that the unsightly, bare dirt be covered over with unsightly cement pavers, resulting in a configuration that did not match its surroundings. I hesitate to call the makeshift walkway a blot on the landscape; the complex of aging, graying government buildings is itself somewhat of a blot. Yet, the path becomes the most appealing part of the landscape when I look at it as a display of human resourcefulness.

Meanderthals are individuals who create desire lines within an established path in order to change direction: "Secondary desire paths adopted by those who are suddenly diverted from their trajectories are, indeed, not aimless but forced re-adjustments."[19]

Past the midway point on the juvenile court path, a fresh desire line appears—a naked one. The roots of a large oak tree have disrupted the pavers so that their threatening edges poke up to create a walking hazard for juveniles and their advocates. Inert concrete is no match for live oak roots. By repeatedly stepping around the hazard, walkers have created a crescent-shaped desire line beside the problem—a short deviation of a few feet leading right back to the paved path. I hope my little truant cousin Katie will likewise find her way back from trouble.

* * *

Every explorer on the World Wide Web is a potential meanderthal, free to create her own journey. While stalking ancestors on the Internet one evening—visiting genealogy sites, checking message boards—I made a sharp turn at Ancestry.com and tripped over something unexpected. The surname Guillory means "powerful desire," combining the Germanic words *wil* (desire) and *ric* (power).[20]

Desire lines are "never perfectly straight. Instead, like a river, they meander this way and that, as if to prove that desire itself isn't linear and [. . .] straightforward."[21]

Uncle John lived to see the renaming of the road that led to his house, but not being an Internet meanderthal, he likely had no awareness of how closely the new name approximated his desire. Guillory of the "powerful desire" is not the same as Desiree the "much desired," but it's close— like a mirror image, or like subject and object. Opelousas officials committed an inadvertent synchronicitous act. Had Uncle John known about the hidden meaning of his name, he would have smiled and maybe even winked. So would our ancestors.

The Problem We All Live With

Josephine, Clara, and Bartholomew

My age was still measured in months and my brother Joe was a toddler when we moved. Mama was apprehensive about abandoning the familiarity of our rented half of an Uptown double shotgun for the promise of a new home in the semi-swampy downtown, downriver, back-of-town part of New Orleans, but the land was so cheap way across town that she and my father could afford to build their own house. I have no memory of living in that Uptown shotgun, but I grew up hearing stories about it: a corner house at the intersection of Josephine and Clara. The distinctly feminine and friendly-sounding street names struck my childish ears like a reminiscence of two nice Uptown ladies. We left the plump, nurturing arms of Miss Josephine and Miss Clara in 1946 and moved to our own home in the 9th Ward, to a street with the masculine-sounding name of Bartholomew.

The move landed us two blocks from the Lone Star Cement Plant where my father and some of our relatives worked. Black labor and white management produced the stuff of sidewalks. The plant was huge, sprawling, many-chambered like a forbidding castle and as gray as wet cement. It rose up and loomed behind the neighborhood, dominating the horizon and dwarfing the smaller factories and warehouses that flanked it on either side. Its highest point was a smokestack that appeared to touch the sky. Boxcars running on tracks laid right in front of the cluster of industries loaded up and thundered off, carrying tons of cement to market. The Industrial Canal flowing behind the plant floated barges of cement to the Mississippi River to join in the shuffle of commerce.

The Lone Star Cement Plant was an entity, one of the things that made for neighborhoodness. The Lone Star Bar was a short walk from the plant gate. A block from the plant, the Desire streetcar dropped workers off early and loaded them back on at day's end for seven cents each way. Blacks and whites boarded the streetcar at the back. Whites moved to the front, Blacks sat or stood in the back.

Cement trucks churning their heavy, wet insides roared past street corners, rolling forward and spinning sideways at the same time, en route to some destination where they spilled their insides upon the earth and created a sidewalk or a house foundation or some other enduring thing. Those trucks were always in a rush, as if fearful that their loads might harden like Lot's wife if they took a second too long to get there with the slush.

An old Italian man who lived next door to us terrorized his grandchildren with a cement myth, telling them that bad children were ground up in cement trucks and sidewalks were made out of them. The children ran home screaming at the sight of the big churning, threatening barrel of a passing cement truck. If the old man called the children in for dinner and they were slow to respond, he just pointed at the nearest slab of sidewalk and they all ran inside, screaming and promising to be good for the rest of their lives.

There really were pieces of children in the sidewalks. We all left traces of our knees and elbows in the pores of the concrete. All of that baby flesh the sidewalks ingested gave them some sort of life. Uncle Freddie, who lived on our block, was a cement finisher, a sculptor of sidewalks and driveways. He told me that "sidewalks have to breathe." For every so many feet of sidewalk, the sculptor had to lay in a flexible strip of asphalt so that the sidewalk could inhale and exhale, expand and contract, thus minimizing the chances of cracks in the concrete. I used to stare at squares of sidewalk, trying to catch them breathing.

The plant whistle blew at exactly twelve o'clock every weekday to signal the lunch break, and the corner grocery filled up with plant workers eating cold cuts and French bread and turning up tall bottles of cold Barq's root beer. Boudreaux's Grocery had a worn, sticky wood-plank floor and a special noontime smell: a mixture of the odor of clean sweat with the aroma of freshly baked French bread, in approximately equal proportions.

Afternoon sun rays streaming through the windows of our house on Bartholomew Street reflected tiny particles of silvery cement dust, little motes that were fine enough to slip through window screens and make the sun rays flicker and dance. My brother and I treated the silver specks like playmates, fanning the glittering sun rays and watching the bright metallic particles make swirls and eddies in the light.

The annual company picnic held on the plant grounds was like a plantation holiday. Workers and their families enjoyed a modest feast at company expense. From a distance, we must have looked like an impressionistic painting: happy families in brightly colored summer clothes, sandals, and straw hats, blurred by a haze of cement dust.

My father came home for lunch most days. Sometimes Uncle Ernest came with him.

Uncle Willie had quit the cement plant before I was born. A doctor told him he had little balls of cement rattling around in his lungs. He moved to Los Angeles to enjoy the sidewalk-free, smog-laden air out there. My cousin James also escaped the plant. He moved to Chicago and became a cab driver.

People routinely set their clocks by the plant whistle and gave daily thanks for their source of livelihood. But quietly, they complained about and commiserated over the fine gray dust that settled on everything, ruining paint finishes, forcing women to dust furniture almost daily, making clothes dry a little stiffer on the line, leaving an imperceptible layer of sidewalk atop every open gumbo pot.

I walked the sidewalks every day, played hopscotch on them, jumped rope on them, scraped knees and elbows on them, measured the seasons by their temperature on my bare feet, studied them to avoid stepping on cracks and lines and thus keep my mother in good lumbar health (*step on a line, break your mother's spine / step on a crack, break your mother's back*), and judged people's economic standing according to whether sidewalk or dirt led to their front doors.

But I didn't associate my father's job at the cement plant with sidewalks. My father, my uncles, and their fellow workers were making the clouds that filled the sky.

Beautiful, fluffy white stuff billowed from the smokestack of the cement plant to form clouds. The clouds floated off and the smokestack made more. Those floated away, more ballooned up. It was a heavenly assembly line. I spent lots of time looking up, watching the clouds form above the smokestack and drift off to decorate the bright blue. Sometimes I could make out animal shapes or human faces, and amazingly, they would change right before my eyes, going from amorphous blobs to faces and then slowly back to blobs, leaving me to search for new recognizable shapes to name. Late in the day, they'd settle on the horizon like vaporous mountains and glow with the sunset. On many days, clouds hung in the whole sky. *The whole sky!* My father and his friends were working especially hard those days, making enough white clouds to fill the sky.

On other, less special days, the smokestack cranked out the white stuff, but the sky couldn't hold it. The white disappeared into dull blue or overcast gray. I had no explanation for these cloudless days, but I was certain it was the sky's fault, not my father's nor the smokestack's. On car trips, I looked out of the window at the clouds, wondering how far they traveled and soon believed that no matter where we went, no matter how far from home, cement plant clouds followed.

My father was doing a very important job: the creation of the things that were somehow associated with the miracle of rain, and that also provided weightless transportation for angels. I spent many hours admiring his work, my feet stuck to the sidewalk, my head in the clouds.

Leona Tate, Tessie Prevost, Gail Etienne, and Ruby Bridges

In 1948, the Desire bus, a big heat-belching hulk, replaced the streetcar named Desire. The fare was still seven cents, but now everyone boarded in front, and Black passengers moved to the rear. Around 1950, the company picnic featured an exotic new food that my brother Joe couldn't wait to get a taste of—canned pork and beans—which he now describes as "one of the greatest disappointments of my childhood."

I started kindergarten at Johnson Lockett Elementary School, the closest separate-but-hardly-equal elementary school, twice the distance to William Frantz—the closest white school. I met up with other children of cloudmakers at Lockett School. Glimmerings of reason forced me to question my smokestack theory. School books pictured exotic places around the world, with names I couldn't even pronounce, and they all had clouds. I struggled to maintain my special place in the cosmos as heir to a cloudmaker, but as I moved from grade to grade in elementary school, I could feel my certainty slipping away. It became difficult and then impossible to sustain the belief that a neighborhood factory that employed my relatives was supplying the entire planet with clouds. I had never discussed my cloud theory with anyone; that the factory made clouds was a truth I held to be self-evident. But at last, reality caught up with me, and I felt like an embarrassment to my-own-self. The factory was making cement. I finally had to admit this. These particular clouds were just the fleeting and purely neighborhood by-product of industry.

My mother put a dust rag in my little hand when I was still a single-digit age. With this rite of passage, I joined the adults in cursing the cement plant, though I was not allowed to say the word "damn" yet—not out loud. No matter. Mama said it often enough for both of us. "Damned dust . . . damned cement plant. Damn, damn, damn!"

The plant continued to make a big nuisance of itself, with its annoying by-product of industry still gushing from the smokestack. I knew now that angels would not ride around on this mess. And as for the miracle of rain, eventually the word "acid" was tacked on to the word "rain." My Aunt Phil would adopt that phrase, saying in her high-pitched voice, "I'm takin' my clothes off the line before the acid rain falls on 'em."

There was widespread resistance to the desegregation of public transportation in the late 1950s, but the vilest backlash to progress was unleashed two years later, when public school desegregation was court-ordered in 1960.

The phasing in of Black students began so modestly that it might have gone nearly unnoticed in some other place at some other time. First-grade classrooms in two public schools were mandated to admit a total of four Black students in November of 1960. Leona Tate, Tessie Prevost, and Gail Etienne entered McDonogh 19 Elementary, a Lower 9th Ward school. Ruby Bridges entered William Frantz Elementary in the Upper 9th Ward. She had attended kindergarten at Johnson Lockett, and with her parents' approval, she was chosen by the school board to enter William Frantz school as its only Black student. A mob of angry whites took over the sidewalk in front of Frantz school. They carried picket signs and waved Confederate flags. They jeered and threw things at the little Black girl.

My brother Joe was in eleventh grade that year, and his weekday trek home included getting off the Galvez bus in front of William Frantz school. As there was no prior announcement of the names of the schools to be desegregated on that November day, he was poised to de-bus at his usual corner, having no idea of what had materialized. Joe was shocked to see the screaming mob as his bus rolled up to that intersection. The driver stopped to let him off, but what they both saw and heard gave them pause. A look passed between them as the white driver's eyes suggested that he might not want to get off the bus there. Joe's eyes agreed, the driver closed the door, and Joe got off the bus at the next stop.

The air we all share had become laden with another kind of pollution. William Frantz school was three blocks over and one block up from our house, yet we could hear the angry chanting in our living room. Day after day, the glittering sun rays that streamed through our windows vibrated with the sound of enraged white citizens: "Two, four, six, eight, we don't want to INTEGRATE!" At some point, Joe noted that members of the mob had misspelled the word "integrate" on their signs, spelling the hated word "INTERgrate." I did not admit to my brother that I, too, spelled the word with an extra "r." The misspelling was understandable. It made sense that such a word contained the concept of "entering" or "intermingling." But rather than admit that I was guilty of the same mistake as the mob, I savored the feeling of being smarter than the bigots.

I caught glimpses of Ruby on television, a neatly dressed little girl crowned with a white ribbon, escorted by armed federal marshals who shielded her from the vicious mob that hurled ugly names and threats and even raw eggs at her. She braved these daily assaults to get to her classroom in which it turned out that she would be the only student. I was in the tenth grade and did not know the little six-year-old girl who lived just blocks from my house, but I was in awe of her bravery and couldn't help wondering to myself whether I could have faced such a challenge, even as a tenth grader. The crushing burden of hope for the future and pain of the past and present shouldered by one so young, so small, seemed out of all human proportion. She was so innocent that on that first day she did not comprehend that anger and hatred and race prejudice were driving the crowd. She thought it was Mardi Gras. She found the chanting of "Two, four, six, eight, we don't want to integrate" to be so catchy that she memorized it and taught it to a neighborhood friend so they could jump rope to it.[22]

Word of the brave little girl spread, and soon Ruby's father was fired from his job, and her grandparents, who were sharecroppers at the time, were evicted from the land they worked.[23]

Yolanda Gabrielle, Pamela Foreman, and Saint Mark

The segregationists had the support of most of our state legislators, who voted repeatedly to usurp the authority of the local school board, close the New Orleans public schools, and withhold salaries for teachers and support staff rather than comply with the judge's order to desegregate. Governor Jimmy Davis, wearing a white cowboy hat, rode his white horse Sunshine up the steps of the state capitol and into the building—a white knight riding to the defense of white supremacy and segregation. The all-white Louisiana Teachers' Association voted to support the governor. For the most part, white parents kept their children out of the two desegregated schools. The boisterous white mob of mostly women dubbed itself "the Cheerleaders," and they carried out their daily racist assault without fear of pushback from anyone in authority. They were the very opposite of those nice uptown ladies, Miss Josephine and Miss Clara.

The Cheerleaders attracted national attention, and suddenly my neighborhood was being reported on by the likes of Walter Cronkite and Chet Huntley. Huntley received death threats because of his coverage of the events. John Cameron Swayze did a live broadcast from a sidewalk outside Frantz school. Television was still somewhat of a new medium then, still finding its voice. As the mob was beamed into living rooms across the nation, the Cheerleaders could be seen and heard abusing children with name-calling that was so offensive that the sound had to be muffled for broadcast. In New Orleans and other Southern cities, television news became a catalyst in social change movements.

The sudden attention from national media felt like an odd collision of fantasy and reality. Back then, "the news" was so un-relatable, so foreign as to seem like fantasy, worlds away from my daily life, while favorite fictions like Lucy and Ricky and Ozzie and Harriet felt real. Now, the news was happening just blocks from my house, and one day I was stunned to see a familiar face on television—a new experience for me—and suddenly the real world was more real. Daisy Gabrielle was featured on the news as the parent of one of the two white students who continued to attend William Frantz School after Ruby Bridges matriculated. Mrs. Gabrielle was a white lady I often saw at the bus stop, or entering and exiting the Florida Housing Project building where she and her family lived, or in Boudreaux's store just across the street from that building.

She was swarthy, with a pleasant demeanor and a soft voice and with enough thick dark hair for two or three hairdos—piled up, pulled back, and hanging all at the same time.

My brother and I were attending different high schools, and my daily transport was the Desire bus, which I boarded at the corner of the Florida Housing Project just yards away from the building where Daisy Gabrielle lived with her husband James and daughter Yolanda. Soon after Mrs. Gabrielle appeared on television expressing her resolve to keep her daughter in school, I was walking up to the Desire bus stop en route to school and came face to face with something ugly and frightening. The high brick wall of the familiar project building where the Gabrielle family lived had been defaced with racist graffiti, jagged Black lettering spelling out threats and racist names. The mob had not squandered all of its venom on Ruby. They saved a huge measure of it for those they considered the worst race traitors: white parents who did not yank their children out of the two integrated schools.

Reverend Lloyd Foreman, pastor of St. Mark's Methodist Church, was another white parent who was vilified and hounded. He had continued to escort his daughter Pamela to Frantz school, and the mob screamed threats and obscenities at the white minister and his little girl every day. John Steinbeck witnessed this scene and wrote that it filled him with "a choked and sickened sorrow."[24] John Updike called the Cheerleaders "segregationist banshees."[25]

Reverend Foreman's church on North Rampart Street, like the Gabrielles' housing project building, was soon covered with racist graffiti. I remember seeing it from a passing car—the green stucco building with beautiful arches now defaced by unholy acts. The Foreman family was forced to move for their own safety.

Some of the white parents who wanted to keep their children in school requested the help of an Uptown group called SOS (Save Our Schools), whose volunteers agreed to provide transportation and escorts for the white students. SOS called their operation the "carlift," but the effort proved to be too dangerous to continue. One morning, the car in which Yolanda Gabrielle was riding was attacked and stoned. Days later, a truck followed the car and tried to ram it. The White Citizens Council compiled a list of names, car descriptions, and phone numbers of everyone involved with the carlift and distributed the list to the mob. This led to threats of death, arson, and disfigurement. The carlift ended and armed federal marshals were called in to escort the children to school.

Yolanda Gabrielle's father, Korean War veteran James Gabrielle—his loved ones threatened at home, at school, and even en route to school, and he himself treated badly at his job—moved his family out of state.

The artist Norman Rockwell felt moved to document Ruby's story visually. In his 1964 painting, she is flanked by four United States Marshals caught in mid-stride against the outer wall of a building marred by the red stains of hurled tomatoes, and with the scrawled word "NIGGER" partially showing. Rockwell titled the painting *The Problem We All Live With*, and it represented a departure from the more neutral Americana the public had come to expect from him. An art site describes Rockwell's signature as part of the message of the painting. The ugly graffiti "parallels the artist's signature below, rendered in mock schoolboy, lowercase penmanship," and the remnants of the tomato could suggest "a visceral burst of skin and pulp that looks like the bloody aftermath of a firing squad."[26]

Soon after the four little girls entered the two previously all-white public schools, the White Citizens Council held a rally that drew over five thousand people. One of the speakers, an elected official, warned the crowd, "Don't wait for your daughters to be raped by these Congolese. Do something about it now." A witness described the rally as "a gathering straight out of Nazi Germany."[27]

The violence spilled over into other parts of the city as roving white vigilante-like groups formed in order to carry out citizens' arrests of Blacks for imagined infractions. Black bus patrons were warned that they should expect random acid-in-the-face assaults and that the same fate awaited any Black people walking in the French Quarter. Avoiding the French Quarter was impossible for me because that was the location of my high school. But for several days, I avoided riding the bus. Uncle Freddie drove me to school and was there waiting for me in his cement-flecked truck when school let out, not exactly an armed federal marshal, but a welcome sight anyway. I escaped assault, but others were not as fortunate. Several Blacks were injured by flying glass when mobs threw bricks through the windows of buses, and two Black citizens were beaten severely. One person was stoned in front of Frantz school.

At the end of the 1960–61 school year, forty-nine white children remained in the city's two integrated schools.[28]

Where was the moral force to counter the ugliness that the whole nation was witness to? The writers John Steinbeck and John Updike wrote about the Cheerleaders, and both wondered where the good white people of New Orleans were. They were here. Just less visible and less successful than the bigots. There were numbers of whites whose decent actions were thwarted because of fear of what other whites would think of them, or because of actual threats. Some parents were visited by, and threatened by, members of the White Citizens' Council. One white mother who returned her child to William Frantz school for a brief time found herself with no friends except for the SOS women who escorted her child to school and the congregation of a Black church that offered help.

There was an anonymous citizen who made loans to the teachers whose salaries had been withheld by the state legislature. There was a group of New Orleans students who carried a petition to the state capitol, asking that the public schools be kept open. Governor Davis refused to meet with them, and his secretary asked the group to reveal the names of the Northerners who paid their expenses. In reality, there was no such link.

Louisiana State University, publicly funded but open only to white students, was the scene of some acts of bravery. Professor Waldo McNeir wrote a letter to the state legislature in which he called their actions "a disgrace and a national scandal." Legislators labeled him a communist. LSU students circulated a petition in support of the professor, but the legislature ignored their efforts, calling the petition "silly nonsense." The investigation of the LSU professor did not proceed, but he was driven to resign anyway, citing "outside threats and inside pressures." The state "authorized a full-scale investigation of the university by the Legislature's Un-American Activities Committee." Fearing reprisals, other LSU faculty members stayed silent, while 329 faculty members at Tulane University, a privately funded white-only institution, signed a statement opposing the investigation and the withholding of public school teacher pay. They also joined with 105 businessmen in calling for the "end to threats, resistance, and demonstrations, the preservation of public education, and a return to the rule of law." Threats and harassment against the educators and businessmen followed.[29]

John McDonogh, William Frantz, and Johnson Lockett

The schools that were the focus of the desegregation battleground were named for local educational advocates. McDonogh 19 Elementary is one of twenty schools named for John McDonogh, a wealthy slave owner who died in 1850. He bequeathed a large portion of his wealth to the New Orleans public schools to serve white children, but also for the benefit of children of free people of color in New Orleans. During his life, he saw to the education of some of his plantation slaves, a practice that the Louisiana legislature designated as a criminal act in 1830. Following the Civil War, French émigré William Frantz became a successful New Orleans businessman. His interest in education led him to serve as a member of the school board for twenty years. One of the duties he most enjoyed was handing out diplomas at graduation ceremonies. Thanks to the advocacy of Ruby Bridges, William Frantz School is listed in the National Registry of Historic Places.

Johnson Lockett was a Black resident of the 9th Ward who was born just after Emancipation. His interest in community matters led him to found the 9th Ward Civic and Welfare League. When the Great Flood of 1927 displaced many white residents of neighboring St. Bernard Parish, Lockett solicited donations of food and clothing and arranged shelter at 9th Ward churches and schools. For six years, I was a student at the school that bears his name. His portrait, displayed in a central part of the building, had eyes that followed you from every angle. In life, those eyes were indeed watchful. Lockett patrolled the 9th Ward regularly, searching out truants and escorting them to school.

Although separated by years, and by race and class, the three men honored in these school names valued education and supported its improvement in their own ways.

9th Ward Civic Relations and Community Improvement Association

The school desegregation era was a terrible, frightening time in our city, but as the years passed, it became common to see Blacks and whites sitting side by side on buses and streetcars, and Black children and white children attended at least some of the schools together. The Cheerleaders ceased showing up to threaten and intimidate children.

Through the rise and fall of all that public hatred, the cement plant remained a neighborhood constant, a silent but guilty witness to human affairs, and by 1970, people were so fed up with plant emissions that they organized. Turning their attention to the air we had to share, Black and white neighbors took up an anti-cloud campaign. Living with the deadly dust gave a different meaning to the title of Rockwell's paintings. Those cement plant clouds came more and more to be seen as not just an annoying by-product of industry but a serious health hazard. The group successfully organized 9th Ward residents who lived in this dust bowl, breathing air we could see and even touch. The lining of those clouds was not silver but rust, lime, clay, and sand—the stuff of cement. The human body is mostly water. What happens when water is mixed with dry cement? In a few generations, we could harden and become a neighborhood of walking pillars of concrete. Would it turn out to be true that sidewalks are made of children?

"This pollution must be stopped!"

"We're sick and tired of this damned cement dust!"

"That white stuff coming out of that smoke stack is killing us!"

"Yeah, and it's ruining the finish on our cars too!"

"We have the right to breathe clean air!"

The Environmental Protection Agency was founded in 1970. That same year, a biracial group, armed only with a sense of justice and a long name—the 9th Ward Civic Relations and Community Improvement Association—set out to make its voice heard. I wonder still whether any of those nice white ladies who spoke up at the 9th Ward CRCIA meetings had been Cheerleaders a decade before, screaming obscenities and threats at little children and feeling perfectly righteous in their actions at the time. Most of the white members of the CRCIA were the right age to have been part of that group.

Around the time that the Association was formed, I met Al, the son of a Cheerleader. We were both in our twenties and had witnessed the school desegregation crisis of a decade before. He and his wife were both raised by racially bigoted parents. Individually, they were protective of family reputations, but they did not hesitate to tell on each other's parents. One day, Al's wife told me that Al's mother had been a Cheerleader. I had never met this woman, but suddenly finding myself associated with her offspring left me feeling as if a mythological monster had fleshed itself out. Al's wife laughed and half-whispered this history while her husband was in the next room. Her lighthearted take on the subject added to my unease.

If any of the white CRCIA had been Cheerleaders, that part of their life stories had been paved over, which was not an impossible thing to achieve. Jimmy Davis, our late governor, provides an example of how easy it can be to rewrite a personal history. The staunch segregationist, white knight astride his steed riding to the rescue of segregation, destroyer of public education, withholder of teacher pay, managed to somehow inspire his obituarist to rehabilitate not only Davis's image but also that of the state he governed. When he died in 2000, his obituary read: "Unlike so many Southern governors, Davis managed the transition [to desegregation] so that, however stormy the rhetoric in the state, there was never any violence or closed schools. . . . He has just never been a demagogue or a hater."[30]

Over several months, the 9th Ward group presented a united front for their just war against air pollution. Members spoke at churches in the area and at the Desire Neighborhood Center, where I was working at the time, having recently graduated from the newly desegregated University of New Orleans. Some of my relatives joined, and soon the group had raised a little army of a respectable size and with a respectful demeanor. They armed themselves with facts, spoke with experts, and presented their demands to plant management. They didn't carry signs with misspelled words, they didn't call people names or foster racial divides; they talked about health and safety and car paint finishes and met with plant representatives several times to make their case on behalf of the neighborhood and the plant workers.

I confess that I had little hope that anything productive would come of their efforts. Growing up in the 9th Ward, I knew that our neighborhood was stigmatized and devalued by many residents of other parts of the city as well as by some of our elected officials. This attitude was directed at white residents of the 9th Ward as well as Black ones, and so when the school board was forced to begin the process of desegregation in two schools, I don't think it surprised anyone that both of the chosen schools were in the 9th Ward. Leading up to the selection of the two schools, members of the school board decided that Black children would be better off in schools with lower test scores so that "they would not feel inferior."[31]

Knowing how low the general regard for our neighborhood ran, I did not expect the residents to be successful in confronting the power behind the cement plant. But I was spectacularly wrong. The campaign was a great success. The peasants banged on the massive castle door and confronted the great, cloud-breathing dragon that ground children of every color into sidewalks. Or, in other words, a huge and hugely expensive filtering system was installed, looking like a new castle chamber grown around the base of the smokestack. The dragon breathed its last. The plant continued to manufacture cement, and the smokestack remained, but with no clouds spewing from its summit, it just stood there like a gigantic retired worker with nothing to do. The damned dust was gone. And just as I had expected, there were still clouds in the sky.

* * *

I received a framed print of Norman Rockwell's *The Problem We All Live With* as a birthday gift some years ago. I had long admired Norman Rockwell's work for its warmth and humor, even though his subjects often left me feeling excluded. His vision of America had seemed to me a whitewashed ideal. But in 1964, Rockwell made Ruby Bridges the subject of one of his paintings. He used the encompassing pronoun "we" in the title, casting the issue of race as an American problem.

That often misspelled word "integrate" tells the story. It comes from the Latin word *integritas*, meaning "to put together parts or elements and combine them into a whole."[32] The word "integrity" derives from the same root. The neighborhood that produced the hateful Cheerleaders also gave birth to the "we" of the 9th Ward Civic Relations and Community Improvement Association when the problem of air pollution was looked at from the detached height of cement plant clouds. For me, that neighborhood organization was the other side of Rockwell's encompassing observation about problems we share.

The battle taken up by the 9th Ward CRCIA was not about race. In fact, its biracial makeup was part of its strength. Blacks and whites suffered equally from the same problem. Working together on a solution led to success.

Those parents who fought such a dirty battle to preserve segregation, even to the point of sacrificing their own children by nearly destroying the whole school system, lived in a state whose educational outcomes ranked second-worst in the nation in 1960. The twenty-first century finds us in third- or fourth-worst position, which can hardly be counted as real progress. Had the Cheerleaders focused even a fraction of their passion on improving public education for all of Louisiana's children, we might all be light years ahead by now.

Today, one can still walk the same sidewalk that the screaming Cheerleaders took over all those years ago. Frantz School is still there. We are still challenged by racial and educational inequities, and Ruby Bridges places her hopes for a better future on children. "Kids come into the world with clean hearts, fresh starts," she said. "If we are going to get through our differences, it's going to come through them."[33]

On November 14, 2014, fifty-four years to the day since she desegregated Frantz School, a statue of Ruby was unveiled there. It features Ruby as a little girl leaning against giant books. It is called *Honoring the Power of Children.*

Missa Luba

It's 1962. My brother is in school in New York. From the Mighty 9—the New Orleans 9th Ward—to the Big Apple. Incredible. He expands my narrow, sixteen-year-old horizon by sending me treasured scraps of his new one: a program book from the Apollo Theater, a Mets hat, letters composed on a typewriter. But the best gift was a record album entitled *Missa Luba,* the Mass sung in Latin by Africans.

At that time, the Mass was celebrated in Latin throughout the world. I suppose I imagined it sounded the same everywhere—organ dirge accompanying classical and operatic Latin echoing off the vaulted ceilings of cathedrals, or sprawled flat on the floor of small churches like ours. The very word "catholic" meant universal, the nuns told us. And no matter the quality of voices or organ, Gregorian chant was soothing in its sameness and monotony.

I had never wondered about Catholicism in Africa. Back then, I don't believe I thought Catholicism even existed in Africa. Our religious instructors generally used the word "pagan" in any sentence that contained the word "Africa." Sometimes the word "missionary" was thrown in as well. But still, I'm sure I never thought about the outcome of missionary work upon "pagan" Africans as resulting in Catholicism, with all of its trappings and rituals. And of course I had no understanding of the history and roots of it all—the colonial and postcolonial stranglehold on Africa that for centuries had been anglicized, catholicized, protestantized, baptized, and pillaged.

I had the tunnel vision of integration in 1962. Integration of the South, of New Orleans, of Canal Street. Africa was as familiar as Mars to my friends and me. The only African roots we acknowledged were those that grew out of our heads. Nappy roots. Naps. That embarrassing condition that was at its worst on the Friday before the Saturday you went to get your hair fixed, or any day that was rainy or humid, or anytime you sweat. New Orleans has an abundance of rain, humidity, and sweat. Naps were a continual challenge.

It was usually in connection with hair that the phrases "the old country" and "the mother country"—phrases borrowed from European immigrants we knew only from television—were used among my friends. If someone looked you in the face and then raised her gaze to your hair and said something about the mother country, you knew this was a friendly though crass reminder that it was time for the hot comb, or maybe a hat. It couldn't have meant any more than that because you both knew you had no mother country.

But then that changed.

Missa Luba gave birth to my mother country.

Here was the familiar Latin, the Mass as known all over the planet. But different. So different. It was African. Clean, clear children's voices, like chimes, melodies with counter melodies floating and dancing above them, the passion of belief in every measure. The chorus throws out a challenge, the solo voice meets it and issues its own challenge. The voices play with phrases, calling and questioning, answering and affirming. They work out their differences and end each song in rich, soul-satisfying harmony. And all of it supported by restless, insistent drums.

It was the drums that did it. I couldn't hear those drums and keep still, no matter how holy the Latin words were. I danced down. I danced like the only Africans I'd ever seen—Black extras in *Tarzan* and *King Kong* movies. I let those drums ripple up my spine and bounce my head up and down while I sang along: *Kyrie eleison, Christe eleison.* This was my first taste of African music, and I knew the words.

I knew the sound, too. In the tension between the chords of the chorus and the assertive, tenorish soloist, I recognized the origins of the sound I knew as "rock 'n' roll" music, the sound that would soon be called "soul" music, and the two-step-three-step-jazz-blues my parents simply called "music."

It was also an undeniably gospel sound.

I wanted to share this experience with my schoolmates. I was certain that if I brought the album to school, our music teacher would see the wisdom of playing it for the class.

Sister Marie Juliette was our buried treasure. With her, for an hour every day, there was respite from algebra, Latin, chemistry, and other tortures. She had been cloistered for some years in a mythical place called Juilliard where the secrets of music were kept. Now, she devoted her days to sharing potent doses of these secrets with us barely worthy rock 'n' roll fans.

Sister Marie Juliette took possession of the *Missa Luba* album and kept it for a suspiciously long time before she finally hinted that she would play it for us one day soon.

On the appointed day, she introduced the album, encouraging our appreciation of the diversity of cultures it represented. The silence of anticipation and curiosity was heavy in the room as Sister let the needle arm slip gently from her plump brown fingers to the spinning record.

The music starts.

Drums and other, unknown percussion instruments begin the tension. The voices of Congolese children join in singing *Kyrie eleison,* familiar Catholic Greek. The tension builds. *Christe eleison.* The drums are relentless. The voices call. In seconds, the room full of Catholic girls are wanton Watusis. Their bodies become percussion instruments. Heads bob, shoulders bounce, hips gyrate, hands clap, fingers pop, forty pairs of saddle oxfords stomp the floor—all this from a sitting position. They know the words. They begin to sing along. Nothing can stop the motion. Nothing except Sister's hand yanking needle arm from record.

The drums die abruptly, and the girls settle back in their chairs. Sister Marie Juliette is disappointed in us. She delivers a short lecture on the sanctity of the music. Then she starts the record again. This time the girls hold out a little longer before they let the dancing Watusi spirits have their bodies. But the Watusis win before the *Kyrie* is over. We are Africans in blue-and-white uniforms, unable to hear our drums without responding.

Sister stops the record again. "This is the Mass," she screams.

I think she called us animals.

* * *

Only my closest friends heard the entire album when they came to my house on weekends.

* * *

The next year, my cousin Joan came to live with us. She joined Ursula, Sylvia, Bernadette, Patricia, Lorraine, Barbara, and me in singing and dancing along with the Catholic Africans. But after a while, Joan began to worry that it might be a sin to dance to the Mass. The rest of us weren't sure, but it felt so good we couldn't stop. There was movement in our hips that even Ernie K-Doe and the Royal Dukes of Rhythm had not evoked, more sensual and satisfying than anything Elvis had stolen. And we weren't giving it up. We danced and sang and shook. *Angus Dei . . . miserere nobis.*

I visualized myself in hell. "What are you in for?" a murderer asks me.

"I did the Watusi to the *Kyrie Eleison*," I confess.

A rapist overhears and gasps at my lack of shame.

Joan worked herself up into minor agony over the guilty pleasure of dancing to the *Missa Luba*. If religion felt this good, it must be sinful. She confessed dancing to the Mass to a progressive young priest. He advised her that Abraham had danced, Isaac had danced, Rebecca and David and a host of Old Testament names had all danced in praise of God. She came home and announced that she was in a state of grace and celebrated by dancing without shame to the *Missa Luba*.

I was grateful to Joan. She sought the counsel that removed the guilt from this pleasure that felt so sinful but that was, in the eyes of this one priest at least, a religious tradition older than Jesus. Ursula and I joined Joan in the dance that day, but I think we all understood that we were not praising God: we were praising Africa and finding her in ourselves.

It seemed odd that I should have found Africa in this roundabout, planetary way, that I first became linked to my motherland by a common religion that is not considered ours.

Catholicism was imposed on Africa by missionaries and imperialists; I belonged to one of the Black Catholic parishes served by priests who called themselves "Missionaries in Service to Colored America," a title which persisted despite the fact that most of the families they ministered to had been Catholic for generations. The words "African" and "Catholic" seemed as uneasy in each other's company as those other two words that described us: "Negro American." What could be more mixed up than Catholic colored girls dancing to African voices and African drums, celebrating the Roman Catholic ritual of sacrifice in a language foreign, classical, and long dead?

Recently, my brother, who's full of obscure, stunning trivia, asked me this: "What type of music would you consider to be the most removed from African musical tradition?"

It didn't take me long to come up with my answer. "Gregorian chant," I said.

"That's what I thought you'd say," he said, smiling. "Gregorian chant," he was pleased to inform me, "originated in Africa centuries ago."

Elementals

Water. Some of my earliest memories are of water.

My childhood awareness was like that of a houseplant—an unconscious living entity that thrives physically as long as its needs are taken care of. Water seeped into some family scenes and forced me into sentience, if only briefly.

A fishing trip jarred me into terrified awareness. I found myself walking in the air, in the space reserved for things with wings. We were headed for a fishing hole in a country town in Louisiana, walking across a narrow train trestle, a frightful structure—railroad tracks impossibly high in the air, held up by a crisscross of giant wooden stilts striding across a great chasm of water fringed by woods. I held onto my father's hand with a sweaty death grip and moved along as fast as I could. I had to concentrate on every step and proceed carefully, as my feet were small enough to slip between the wooden cross ties that supported the metal rails. Between each hunk of wood was air. Far below, water. Off to the sides, treetops. I was looking down at treetops.

I had awakened in some kind of hell.

The adults, toting fishing gear, wondered aloud about the time of day. A train was due soon, they said.

"Shhh, I think I hear a train whistle."

They laughed. They speculated about which direction the train would come from. I could see that a train coming from either direction meant that we'd have no place to go except straight down. The adults—my parents, aunt and uncle, assorted cousins—found this funny. We were all at risk of returning to our watery origins, violently, from a great height. And they were laughing.

Apparently, we survived.

The tracks and trestle were real, but the train was a figment. I don't remember the fishing part of the fishing trip or the return trek across the trestle. I must have slipped back into the primordial security of houseplant consciousness to escape the incomprehensible adult world.

At some point, I experienced another water-induced moment of distress, but this time it was vicarious. I was learning empathy. Visiting family in rural Louisiana, I witnessed a strange ritual. Families gathered around a pond as some adults, waist-deep in water, repeatedly dunked people below the surface. Why? What had those people done to deserve this? I could clearly see terror on their faces as they surfaced, gasping for air, only to be cruelly submerged again.

Why was everyone else standing around watching so quietly instead of saving these poor wretches? It was as inexplicable as it was unforgettable.

* * *

Fire figured in some early memories, too. My father blueprinted and built our house in such a way that fire glowed at its center for the six cold months of the year. In the square hall in the middle of the house, a furnace was recessed into the hardwood floor. The hall was so small that the furnace took up most of its floor space. Blue-gold flames glowed below a rectangular metal grate that became untouchably hot when the furnace was aflame. There was space to step around it to get from room to room. You could walk on the grate if you were wearing shoes, and if your legs were long enough, you could leap it in one bound. You could even defy the flames and hotfoot across the grate in sock feet. Then you could savor the lingering glow that stuck to the bottoms of your feet like honey.

The bedroom, living room, and bathroom doors all opened into the hall where the furnace lived. On a cold day, wearing thick-soled shoes, you could go into the hall, close all of those doors, stand on the furnace grate, and let the billowing heat from the quiet fire envelope you and make you feel like bread in a toaster. "Hogging the heat," my mother called it. You could hog the heat for a long moment without getting crispy. The slight whiff of burning shoe sole was your signal to get out of the toaster. *Now!*

The floor furnace was our family hearth, the fire that comforts without consuming. But I remember two different times of the dampening of the hearth, when the four of us—Mama, Daddy, my brother Joe, and me—stood around the floor furnace with our feet in water.

In one of those scenes, my parents are arguing. I am filled with fear, hearing anger in their raised voices. In the other scene, there is water on the floor, and my parents are not arguing but instead talking in serious tones as we all stand around the floor furnace on damp feet.

The memories are so dreamlike that, for a long time, I wondered if this odd mixing of fire and water really happened. But I recall that when I became aware of my family in that setting a second time, I thought to myself, *It's happening again.* Confirmation would come years later.

* * *

Fire and water cohabitated in the attic of our house. My father had installed the water heater in a low-slung perch up there. A trap door, high up on a kitchen wall, gave access to the heater's controls and offered a peek at its eternal blue flame. The two elements, along with their natural gas host, coexisted as productive allies in their tubular metal housing, until the water heater grew rust and began to leak. The house and its infrastructure were the same age I was, and once we reached our thirties, just as I was establishing myself as an independent adult, the water heater aged past its prime. It would have to be replaced, an expensive proposition.

My mother's lament over this latest homeowner heartache triggered memories of those powerful early images of water around the hearth. I had long since resolved the terror of the train trestle episode. There'd been no threat of an oncoming train. I had come to understand, even appreciate the strange humor my relatives had indulged in. I could look back at that terrified little girl with the tiny feet and point at her and laugh. I had long since made peace with the baptismal dunking, too. My Baptist father came from a tradition that held that sin had to be washed away almost literally with an abundance of water. For my Catholic mother, the water was more symbolic; a mere sprinkle was adequate.

But those other highly strange family scenes around the furnace had left a trail of wet footprints as they stalked me into adulthood. Suddenly I needed to give voice to the dreamlike visions that were at once vague and vivid.

Mama and I were sitting at her kitchen table, commiserating over the quiet drip-drip of the old water heater just above us. Though I felt reluctant to revisit the memories, I braced myself and changed the subject. I described my childhood memories to my mother, starting with the frightening one of fire, water, and discord where she and my father were yelling at each other—my only memory of an argument between them. I painted the scene for her in a halting voice, uneasy about where my quest might lead. Would my questions trigger a wave of sad memories for my mother? Or renewed anger? She listened intently and then, to my amazement, she laughed.

"You remember that?" she asked me. "You were so little. . . . How could you remember that?"

"I think I remember it because it scared me so."

"Well, the reason we were arguing was that I was trying to keep your daddy from killing your brother. Joe had flushed all kinds of things down the toilet, just to watch them swirl around and disappear. He kept on finding things to flush—wash rags, socks, just anything—until the toilet stopped up and overflowed and flooded the bathroom, the hall, and the floor furnace."

"So we really were standing in water? Toilet water?"

"Yes. And the water had actually put out the fire in the floor furnace."

I laughed, relieved to know that the reason for my parents' argument was sordid only in the sense that the water at our feet had come from the toilet. And Daddy would not have killed Joe. My mother was a born storyteller, fond of hyperbole. She said that Daddy wanted to whip Joe, and she didn't want him to do so in anger. She wanted him to calm down before deciding what to do about Joe and his latest experiment.

Joe lived, and he didn't even get his promised whipping.

"And was there another time?" I asked Mama. "I remember a time when the four of us were standing around the floor furnace with all of the hall doors closed, and you and Daddy were talking but not arguing. I remember water on the floor that time too."

"Yes, there was another time," Mama said. "That was the time your daddy came home from duck hunting dripping wet because his pirogue had turned over in the marsh. It was a cold-cold day. He came in the house freezing, dripping water everywhere. We closed all of the hall doors, and he stood over the floor furnace taking off his wet clothes, trying to dry off and get warm."

Our smiles faded slowly, and we both sank down into a river of quiet thoughts—private thoughts—yet I knew we were thinking about the same thing. We were remembering another winter hunting trip, when my father was again in pursuit of ducks, creatures at home in both air and water. I was six years old, and my brother was eight. Daddy's pirogue, that treacherous, narrow little dugout excuse-for-a-boat, betrayed him once again, turned over and delivered him into the cold, deep, marshy fringes of Lake Pontchartrain. But this time, he was not able to surface. He did not come home cold and wet to seek the warmth of hearth and family. He would never come home again.

* * *

Many years later, I understand why I held on to those early watery memories. They were warnings. It was as if the spirit of water, with its power to extinguish life's fire, had tried to prepare us for a loss that it did not have the power to prevent. Recognizing this, I suddenly felt a deep connection to water's very soul, as if I had discovered an ally who'd been there all along, unnoticed.

Sadness still bobs up and down like driftwood. Bitterness has been washed away.

PART THREE

The Trail of Rice

You got rice cooked?

This question always came in connection with a gift of food, something so savory, hearty, so dense with flavor that it needed the gastronomic tempering of rice.

Stopping by my mother's or one of my aunt's on my way home from work often netted me a lagniappe portion to go: a container of beans—red, white, or green—or gumbo, or some beef or pork or chicken, stewed simmered smothered braised, all spicy, garlicky, oniony, bellpeppery, parsley-y and gravy-y. That question, *You got rice cooked?*, always came just before or just after I was handed something delicious that was destined to top a mound of rice or to have a healthy scoop of rice sunk into it. And if the answer to that question was *no*, the additional gift of some cooked rice was always thrown in.

Rice supports the food needs of multitudes worldwide, and it pervades the lore and customs of cultures that rely on it. Hawaiians say "go home, cook rice" at the end of the workday to acknowledge their intent to head home and start dinner. It is such a widely used expression that it shows up on T-shirts and mugs.[34] The Filipino language has seven words for rice.[35] The Thai cook says "eat rice" when calling the family to a meal. In the Chinese language, the word for rice is the same as the word for food, and a common Chinese greeting translates as, "Have you had your rice today?"

I celebrate rice in all its forms, except for rice pudding, just the thought of which gives me bad school cafeteria flashbacks. Rice pudding is just wrong, and everyone in my family shuns it.

Perfect rice means evenly cooked grains that stand apart from one another. In India, this quality is likened to the ideal relationship between brothers—"close, but not stuck together."[36] I learned to cook rice at a young age. Mama taught me the index finger method:

Index Finger Method of Cooking Rice

> *Put two coffee cups of rice in the rice pot. Rinse it a few times, pouring off the water until it's almost clear. Add fresh water, enough to cover the first joint of your index finger as you touch the surface of the rice. Add a pinch of salt. Boil uncovered until water is absorbed. Lower the heat, put the lid on, and cook until rice is tender.*

In Louisiana, rice is celebrated at an annual festival in a small Cajun town called Crowley, the Rice Capital of the World.[37] Some years ago, I attended a conference there along with a small group of New Orleanians. All other participants were from Crowley and its environs. Our conference packets included a store coupon for a bag of rice, and during a lull in the program, some of the Crowley folks swarmed around us and tried to talk us out of our rice coupons. They spoke as if no one outside of their rice mecca would know what to do with a bag of rice. I was surprised—not by the fact that they approached us like sweet-talking junkies but by their assumption that New Orleans people were not rice junkies too. We presented our credentials in the form of names of rice dishes we were known for, and they reluctantly accepted us as members of their tribe, begrudgingly walking away, leaving us clutching our precious coupons.

I was born in New Orleans, which, compared to Crowley, may have a somewhat less intense love affair with rice, but the rice pride here is thick. My mother was born and raised in Opelousas, another Cajun town where life would have no meaning without rice. Opelousas is famous for one of my favorite foods: boudin, a spicy pork-and-rice mixture stuffed into a sausage casing and then steamed. It is virtually a meal in a tube, and in Cajun country, it is said that a seven-course meal consists of a yard of boudin and a six-pack of beer.

In a way, I identified with the rice-based elitism of those Crowley residents. Rice snobbery is rampant in my family. "All that good gravy and no rice to put it on"—this is a put-down of the shortsighted, culturally deficient host. No matter how good the meal might otherwise be, the absence of rice is unforgivable if gravy is involved. Rice and gravy go together like . . . well . . . like rice and gravy. Missing-in-action gravy is another offense. Unless something like beans or smothered okra will grace the rice, tasty gravy is a must. The cook who serves meat and leaves the rich, browned pan drippings behind—the gravy in its embryonic state—is culinarily impaired. As for the skill level of the rice cook, my people are unmerciful. S/he who turns out mushy rice is universally denounced. And underdone, crunchy rice (*good God!*) sends little electric shocks through one's very bones. The offender will be judged harshly for such an abomination. I think these harsh ad hominem/womanem attacks are entirely justified.

Rice is an important part of life here, but it seldom comes up as a topic of discussion, unless it is somehow implicated in a disastrous meal somewhere. A while back, I learned that I know very little about rice as a crop or as a commodity, despite its constant presence in my life. In googling a recipe, I happened upon a site that included some history about its featured rice dishes. The writer briefly described the African roots of rice cultivation and its connection to the enslavement of Africans in the American colonies. In a community where the white settlers were nearly starving, a colonial official commissioned two slave ships to fetch captives from the rice-growing region of West Africa. I did not know that the ordering up of certain Africans with such specificity was an established practice. Such an arrangement cast the ungodly transaction as something akin to ordering merchandise from a catalog, but on a massive scale.

Yet the thing that sustained my interest was learning that the technology for growing rice has African origins. The coastal area from Senegal to Sierra Leone was called the Rice Coast, not for the crop alone, but also for the ancient knowledge of the cultivation and processing of the crop. Africa, where humankind was born, where great civilizations flourished for centuries, was reduced by traders to the names of its exploitable resources—the Pepper Coast, the Grain Coast, the Ivory Coast, the Gold Coast, the Slave Coast, the Rice Coast.

Historians have so muddled the origins of rice technology in the New World that Africa's contributions have been either ignored or distorted, leaving us with the misconception that enslaved Africans provided nothing more than a pool of unskilled labor to be exploited by American colonists, who are canonically credited with the creation of the complex system of rice cultivation.

I've never seen a rice field up close, but on car trips through farm country, I learned to identify the fields of floppy, tall green grass as the revered Louisiana crop. I didn't know that rice roots thrive in water until the Vietnam War era, when news coverage showed scenes of American soldiers bearing arms, slogging shin-deep through rice paddies where Vietnamese farmers in straw hats bent over the water to slip little green shoots into the muddy bottom, restarting the life cycle of the crucial crop.

Rice is ancient. Archeologists surmise that it was in the watery areas of West Africa that the species *oryza glaberrima* was first domesticated 3,500 years ago. For her book *Black Rice*, Judith Carney searched through early documents in which African rice cultivation is described by traders and other visitors. Some of those early accounts included diagrams of complex irrigation systems. Islamic scholars traveling to the Mali Empire described rice cultivation along the Niger Delta in the fourteenth and sixteenth centuries. European explorers wrote about rice cultivation in Africa and commented on the many seed varieties in use in 1455. Documents from 1480 show Portuguese ships purchasing rice from African traders.[38]

Since rice needs wet roots during certain periods and dry roots at other times, water control is crucial. Too much water is as detrimental as too little. African farmers developed seed varieties and agricultural methods to accommodate different terrains, and they staggered harvest times to achieve multiple yields. For centuries, these farmers raised enough rice to feed their communities and to have surplus rice for trade. They used three major methods: the upland system, known as dry rice cultivation, and two wet rice systems: the inland swamp terrain system and the tidal irrigation system. All of this knowledge was handed down over generations just as, on a small scale, my mother taught me the rice-cooking method she learned from her mother.

In the upland system, planting coincides with the rainy season. The rain fed-rice, as it's called, thrives in its seasonal wetland. Farmers dig drainage channels to control water levels, and the ripened grain is ready for harvest during the dry season. Inland swamp cultivation makes use of areas where groundwater and rainwater can be tapped to create reservoirs. Engineering techniques control water levels and drainage. Tidal, or coastal, rice cultivation takes advantage of water from rivers and estuaries along coastal areas. An additional challenge of the tidal method is the controlling of saltwater encroachment and tidal flow as ocean currents push into rivers and estuaries. African rice farmers built embankments to prevent tidal inundation of their rice fields. They constructed fresh water reservoirs to dilute the ocean salt before tidal water flowed into the fields. For wet rice cultivation, a complex, watery maze of embankments, canals, ditches, valves, and sliding gates manage water levels in order to flood and drain the rice fields as needed. One of the many impressive features is a system of valves that allows floodgates to open and close automatically with the rising and falling tide. In this way, the natural ebb and flow of tides work to maintain the correct water level in the rice fields. African farmers who engineered these systems could tend to other chores, or spend time at home with their families while the tides quietly assisted with rice production.

In some areas, cattle graze in drained rice fields between planting seasons, allowing the soil to rest and to be fertilized. In other areas, farmers keep their reservoir water level high and stock it with fish that are ready for harvesting before the next planting.

By the seventeenth century, the ancient knowledge and technology had found their way across the ocean with the Atlantic slave trade. The terrain of some coastal areas of the colonies was similar to that of the Rice Coast of Africa, and the crop flourished in the New World. A plantation owner described the transformation:

> With an expenditure of energy that rivaled the labor required to construct the pyramids of Egypt, enslaved workers built a system of earthen embankments, canals, sluiceways and gates, transforming the rice plantations into what one planter called a "huge hydraulic machine [. . .] requiring skill and unity of purpose to keep in order."[39]

American planters also adopted crop rotation methods seen in African rice cultivation. In South Carolina, cattle grazed in dry rice fields, and today in Louisiana, crawfish flourish in wet rice fields.

Slave ships out of Rhode Island, New York, Connecticut, Massachusetts, and the Carolinas, as well as parts of England, fetched captives from the Rice Coast, and rice culture spread to Louisiana, Georgia, Virginia, Florida, New Jersey, and the Carolinas, becoming most profitable in South Carolina. The majority of the enslaved Africans arriving in the colonies entered through the port of Charleston, South Carolina. Planters requested and paid higher prices for Africans from the Rice Coast, who made up the largest group purchased in South Carolina and Georgia in the eighteenth century. A Charleston newspaper of the time advertised the arrival of "a choice cargo of windward [Rice Coast] [...] negroes who have been accustomed to the planting of rice."[40] Some of the ships that docked in Charleston were unable to sell Africans from non-rice-growing areas and had to sail off to other ports in search of profits.

Demand for rice grew as West Indian sugar plantations imported it from South Carolina for slave food, and European markets began to favor the "Carolina gold" over other varieties of the grain. In 1699, two thousand barrels were shipped to England; in less than two decades, that amount rose to fifteen thousand barrels. The cycle of production and wealth accumulation continued and rice stores overflowed, becoming so bountiful that the governor of the state complained that there were not enough ships to carry off all of the rice to international markets.

A planter named Charles Manigault, described as a French-speaking cosmopolitan gentleman capitalist, bought a South Carolina rice plantation in 1833 for $49,500, and in less than thirty years, it was valued at $266,000.[41] (In today's equivalent value, the original investment would be $1,414,285.00, growing to $5,018,867.00 in under thirty years.[42]) Manigault called his plantation his gold mine.

More wealth for plantation owners led to increased importation of African rice farmers to provide expertise and free labor. In the 1730s, about 12 percent of South Carolina's enslaved Africans were from the Rice Coast; by the 1770s, the number had risen to 64 percent.[43] At the beginning of the eighteenth century, there were 2,444 Africans in South Carolina; thirty years later, there were twenty thousand, with Africans outnumbering whites two to one.[44] As one planter described the progression, "Rice is raised so as to buy more Negroes, and Negroes are bought so as to get more rice."[45]

Rice is enshrined in the founding document of our nation.[46] Delegates to the Constitutional Convention argued over many issues that directly impacted slavery. Debate arose over whether to tax imports and exports, namely the importing of enslaved persons and the exporting of the crops they produced, which at the time meant rice and tobacco. Delegates from Southern states would not accept any taxation and threatened secession, and they found allies in delegates from New England who represented the interests of the "'carrying trade'"—shippers of "rice and other products produced by slave labor."[47] In the end, the slaving interests among the founding fathers got their way and made taxing themselves unconstitutional.

* * *

Many historians have ignored all of the evidence for the origins of rice seed and technology and instead approached the subject like an interesting puzzle. Since rice was not native to North America, they sought an explanation for its sudden appearance and the great success of the crop in the colonies. One man cooked up the social equivalent of rice pudding with this story:

> The first white people that came to this country hardly knew how to get their living here. They did not know what would grow best in this country. . . . But there was a wise man in South Carolina. . . . His name was Thomas Smith . . . [and he] had once lived in [*sic*] a large island thousands of miles away from South Carolina. In that island he had seen the people raising rice. He saw that it was planted in wet ground. He said that he would like to try it in South Carolina. But he could not get any seed rice to plant. The rice that people eat is not fit to sow.
>
> One day a ship came to Charleston . . . from the large island where Smith had seen rice grow. The captain of this ship was an old friend of Smith. Thomas Smith told the captain that he wanted some rice for seed. . . . The cook had one little bag of seed rice. The captain gave this to his friend.
>
> There was some wet ground at the back of Smith's garden [where] he sowed some of the rice. It grew finely. He gathered a good deal of rice in his garden that year. He gave part of this to his friends. They all sowed it. The next year there was a great deal of rice. After a while the wet land in South Carolina was turned to rice fields. Every year many thousands of barrels of rice were sent away to be sold. All this came from one little bag of rice and one wise man.

This account is called "One Little Bag of Rice" and has a copyright date of 2007–2011 at the website of Heritage History, but the original account goes back to 1731. That year, Captain Fayrer Hall, a "veteran north American trader" and commander of the *Sea Nymph*, published *The Importance Of The British Plantations In America To This Kingdom*, in which he claimed that the chance arrival of seed rice occurred in 1685.[48] Over the years, many have rewritten Hall's story, with some writers naming the origin of the seed as India or China or Madagascar and with at least one writer denying that Madagascans are African. The name of the heroic colonist has also fluctuated somehow, with writers replacing Thomas Smith with Henry Woodward or with a group of unnamed colonists.[49] But the basics of the story have not changed: that the arrival of seed rice in the colonies was a chance occurrence, the recipient one or more wise white men whose ingenuity resulted in the great success of the crop and great wealth for the colonists.

Historians at the Institute for Southern Studies note that during the rice plantation era, planters began writing histories of South Carolina rice cultivation and that these "historians had taken up the theme with the usual show of erudition if not always with the strictest attention to accuracy."[50] Going on three centuries later, the story of "one little bag" persists and is treated as history by contemporary entities like American Rice Incorporated and The South Carolina Department of Agriculture.[51]

Judith Carney provides an alternative explanation, one that makes infinitely more sense. Harvested rice had to be dried and milled in order to be edible. Once the husk is removed, the rice cannot be used for seed. African women were skilled at husking rice with a wooden mortar and pestle and at winnowing the grain using handmade baskets. Unhusked rice was taken aboard slave ships and processed by the captive women to prepare it for feeding slaves and crew. Unhusked rice is seed rice, and it traveled with the human cargo along with the wooden tools and handmade baskets, which were also adopted by colonial planters.[52]

The cultivation of rice in the New World did not come about by accident, as these myths imply. Such a major undertaking had to be based on some calculated decision-making. A 1995 *Ebony* magazine article acknowledges African innovations in early American farming, quoting a Virginia governor who, in 1648, ordered the colonists to plant rice "on the advice of 'our Negroes,' who said that conditions in Virginia were as favorable to the production of the crop as 'in their country.'"[53]

Eventually, descendants of the planter class dug deep to support their claims. The little-bag-of-rice folktale neglected to account for rice technology or slavery. It was assumed that the technology sprang from the heads of the planters and that slavery was barely a footnote to the enterprise. Even though planters requested and paid high prices for Africans from the Rice Coast, they marveled at the West African engineering feats that were successfully transplanted to the colonial coast. One historian even looked to China to explain the technology.

In 1937, nearly three centuries after the little-bag-of-rice story first appeared, Duncan Clinch Heyward, in *Seed from Madagascar,* concluded that colonial rice planters studied Chinese paintings of rice fields and that this somehow led them to copy their complex technology for growing rice. Without presenting any evidence, the historian imagined a scene three hundred years before he himself was born: Carolina planters gathered around paintings of water buffalo plowing Chinese rice fields, causing these ancestors to experience an odd *aha!* moment. This pseudo-theory is harder to swallow than a heaping second helping of rice pudding. Food historians Robert M. Weir and Karen Hess point out that the colonial plantation system and the Chinese system "were quite dissimilar."[54]

Nevertheless, Duncan Clinch Heyward's gazing-at-Chinese-paintings theory, his imagining the imaginings of long-dead others, took hold and lives on in the twenty-first century. The South Carolina Department of Agriculture's web page from 2011 buys it: "Methods used by the Chinese and the colonists were very similar, because the colonists copied Chinese prints to plant and cultivate rice."[55]

Carney points to racial prejudice as a reason why so many erroneous theories have gone unchallenged. That bias gave rise to the presumption that the development of technology was beyond the ability of Africans as well as the "belief that Africans failed to domesticate crops, a step crucial for the emergence of civilization."[56] Those assumptions began to crumble when rice seed samples gathered from both Asia and Africa in the early nineteenth century were re-examined in 1855. Asian rice, *Oryza sativa,* had been considered the only rice species. But a German scientist named Ernst Gottlieb examined the Asian and African samples and discovered that they were two distinct species. Gottlieb was able to show that domesticated African rice was cultivated from a wild variety that was indigenous to Africa, just as Asian rice was domesticated from a wild Asian parent. He named the African variety *Oryza glaberrima.*

Some historians responded with, *OK, if we can't have China, we'll take Portugal,* sort of. Twentieth-century European agricultural scientists acknowledged that the traditional African rice culture was similar to that of the New World rather than to that of China, but they surmised that it was Portuguese traders who taught rice technology to African farmers. No evidence for such a claim has been put forward, and Judith Carney asks how a civilization that was not known for rice cultivation could have taught it to others. Answering her own question, she suggests that a mindset of racial bias lies behind such flawed conclusions.[57]

Accounting for the role of slavery in rice production, David Doar, planter descendant and historian, probably represented the thinking of his class when he praised the "engineering ability" displayed by "everyday planters [who] laid out these thousands of fields and tens of thousands of banks and ditches" and dismissed the African contribution as the unskilled labor of "intractable negro men and women, but lately brought from the jungles of africa [*sic*]."[58]

Many contemporary sources make the same case, albeit a little more delicately. The South Carolina Department of Agriculture writes that "planters developed a highly effective hydraulic system for flooding and draining the fields, even though almost all of the other work was done by hand, creating a new reliance on slavery."[59] American Rice Incorporated likewise relegates the contributions of Africans to unskilled labor: "Rice farming's extremely high hand-labor requirements are credited with having started the plantation era of the Southern States."[60] Things are changing. The work of more recent historians is reflected in some accounts of the trail of rice, although it's a bit grudging in some cases. The History Channel webpage says, "planters in coastal South Carolina (perhaps aided by the skills of their slaves) took up rice cultivation."[61] The Gilder Lehrman Center for the Study of Slavery, Resistance, and Abolition at Yale University writes, "The slaves may also have contributed to the system of sluices, banks, and ditches used on the South Carolina and Georgia rice plantations."[62]

* * *

An accurate history of rice in the New World is still being written, but there is widespread agreement that the rice trail that leads from the slave ship to the kitchen has left African footprints that are still evident. Rice and bean dishes have long been staples of West Africa. Food historians have observed that all of the formerly slave-holding areas have some popular version of a rice and legume dish.[63] If New Orleans were a country, its national dish would be red beans and rice. Hoppin' John, made of black-eyed peas and rice, is a favorite in the Carolinas, and a similar Caribbean dish is called rice and peas. Black beans and rice is a staple in Cuba, pinto beans and rice in Mexico.

These foods are so much a part of their respective cultures that they show up as figures of speech in the languages. In Brazil, rice and beans are so central to everyday life that the expression "*arroz com feijão*" is used to refer to the fundamentals or basics of anything.[64] Our three Rs would be the rice and beans of education in Brazil. Huey Long, who served as governor of Louisiana from 1928 to 1932, reportedly described the impossibility of vouching for the racial purity of white people in his state by saying that all of the "'pure whites' in Louisiana could be fed 'with a nickel's worth of red beans and a dime's worth of rice.'"[65] The word "zydeco," the name for Black Cajun music, comes from the French word for beans: *les haricots*. "Gumbo yaya," two African words meaning *okra* and *rice*, has come to refer to the confusion of many people talking at once.[66]

Back in 1797, George Washington acknowledged the vital role of Africans in plantation kitchens. "The running off of my cook," he wrote, "has been a most inconvenient thing to this family." Washington hired slave catchers to hunt the cook down, but all attempts were unsuccessful.[67]

Misfortune of a much greater magnitude than one missing cook befell the kitchens and fields of the planter class sixty-six years later: "A crisis is upon us which demands the development of the *will* and *energy* of Southern character. The race of good cooks among us is almost extinct" (emphasis in original).[68] So wrote E. W. Warren of Macon, Georgia, in 1872. The crisis he wrote of is otherwise known as the Emancipation Proclamation. According to Karen Hess and Robert M. Weir, this theme of facing up to domestic crisis dominated post-Emancipation cookbooks as the privileged class tried to cope.

In the fields, rice plantation owners tried to adapt to what was euphemistically referred to as "lack of efficient labor," but the issue was not just the loss of free labor. A planter with fifty years of experience as a rice grower tried to raise a crop in 1881 without Africans and found himself unable to direct the enterprise or train workers. As the planter put it, before Emancipation, "the younger ones were then being trained by the parents and the very efficient foremen."[69] Weir and Hess write that grain cultivation "requires generations of continuing experience" and "various skills of high sophistication."[70] During the plantation era, enslaved African rice farmers transformed the landscape. In South Carolina alone, they cleared over forty thousand acres of land and dug 780 miles of canals by the beginning of the 1800s.[71] With that base of knowledge and experience lost to the planter class, rice production swiftly declined in the former colonies.

An African proverb says, "Every time an old man dies, a library burns down." The proverb could apply to rice cultivation and cuisine in the new world. Emancipation was like a death to the planter class, causing them the loss of connection to the great African rice library that had kept them wealthy and well fed.

* * *

In Louisiana, where mechanized methods had already been introduced, rice went from a minor to a major crop, and today the state is the third-largest rice producer in the nation. But prior to Emancipation, Louisiana planters relied on the same slave-based system as their counterparts in other states. Seeking to explain how our state got into large-scale rice production, some of our historians tell a colorful story:

> Louisiana's distinctive method of producing river rice was discovered by accident during New Orleans' early years. During a hurricane a storehouse containing rice was destroyed and the grain stored there for use as food was thoroughly scattered. After a while there appeared at the edge of the backswamp a good stand of rice which was harvested and consumed. So, Louisianians learned to plant at the lower edge of the natural levee's backslope in time to take advantage of the spring flood. . . .[72]

I have personally named this account "Gagging on Rice Pudding on the Banks of the Mississippi." This little tale does not specify whether the stored rice was already milled, but it does say that the rice was to be "used as food." That implies that it was milled, or husked, rice—the grain in its edible state—not seed rice. Husked rice will not germinate, no matter how strong the hurricane winds that scatter it.

The late Marcus Christian, New Orleans poet, historian, and educator, examined some of Louisiana's antebellum documents. In his unpublished manuscript *The History of The Negro in Louisiana*, he quotes from a 1718 document in which a slave-trading company was commissioned to deliver "three or four hogsheads of rice for planting and a few Negroes who knew how to cultivate it."[73] Thus began rice cultivation in Louisiana. After that first shipment, almost all of the Africans brought to Louisiana were natives of the rice-growing region of Africa. "These skills were so vital to Louisiana settlers that slave ship captains were instructed not to stop in the West Indies en route to Louisiana because French West Indian planters would buy up all their 'cargo,' leaving none for Louisiana colonists."[74]

Many contemporary academic writers have taken up the subject of Africa's contributions to America's rice culture and economy. Judith Carney traveled to rice regions in North and South America and West Africa and published *Black Rice* in 2001; she built on the research of Daniel Littlefield and Peter Wood,[75] who investigated and wrote about the subject in the 1970s. Edda L. Fields Black, an African American descendant of South Carolina rice farmers, published *Deep Roots: Rice Farmers in West Africa and the African Diaspora* in 2008; she found herself peeling leeches from her legs while slogging knee-deep in African rice fields, learning the culture firsthand.[76] Food historian Jessica B. Harris traveled extensively to connect clues for her books on the spread of African foodways in the New World. Robert M. Weir and Karen Hess collected and analyzed recipes for their 1992 book *The Carolina Rice Kitchen*, which includes much information on Africa's role in the field and in the kitchen. All of these writers use evidence and research to present their case for Africa, while the historians who cling to their odd myths lack facts to back them up.

Carney quotes a geography professor and researcher whose 1962 article lists several nations that contributed to the international food pantry. The professor declared that "Africa [. . .] provided nothing important."[77] That, again, is a load of rice pudding. Rice was the first crop to be traded globally,[78] and along with other African exports, it changed the world. Our modern food culture might be quite different without peanuts, coffee, sesame seeds, the kola nut—the basis for cola drinks—and deep fat frying in peanut oil, just to name a few of Africa's gifts to the world.[79]

Planters and their descendants who told their stories, and even agricultural scientists, may have begun with that assumption, that Africans contributed nothing. If that was their starting point, it might explain the imaginative accounts that resulted. Is that how we inherited the evidence-free stories of a chance gift of seed rice, and planters gazing at Chinese paintings in the Carolinas, and a providential hurricane in Louisiana? In 1945, historians at the Institute for Southern Studies reviewed and published documents left by a South Carolina planter. The historians caution that

> [. . .] the most truthful of men do not always practice in private what they advise in print; and it is always necessary to remember that while slavery was under attack the authors of these writings were strongly tempted to claim for the plantation system every possible merit. [. . .] Until a solid basis of this kind of documentary evidence is provided, the rice-plantation tradition will be in danger of suffocation at the hands of sentimentalists.[80]

* * *

Some years ago, I made an innocent observation at a gathering of friends: that the New Orleans shotgun house was African in origin. My friend Conrad protested and repeated the common wisdom about shotgun pellets fired through the front door, traveling through every room and exiting the back door without hitting anything—hence the name. I had heard that my whole life just as he had.

Then Conrad said he was tired of me. He said something like, "You sixties Black people—you learn a little African history, and then you try to claim everything came from Africa."

I can't remember now if it was the architecture or the word "shotgun" that I was claiming for Africa, but I knew I had read or heard something somewhere. I couldn't cite a source for my friend, and even if I could have, I was unable to talk because I was doubled over laughing.

Conrad is a very liberal white New Orleanian, and I had strained the limits of his good nature by challenging his heritage: the classic Creole cottage. He wasn't having it, and his reaction was so unexpected that I couldn't help laughing. I also felt he had defined me pretty well, and I found that funny, too.

I had gone through all those years of school without learning anything positive about Africa and had only come to learn about that part of my heritage when 1960s people took up the subject with righteous zeal. I was well into my twenties before I learned that "gumbo" is an African word for okra, and that the ancient Egyptians did not look like Charlton Heston, or that the root word for "okay"—perhaps the most American word in our lexicon—comes from an African language. I'm not so zealous in public any more, but I am still interested in seeing the role of Africans more widely acknowledged and respected in American and global culture. The trail of rice seems a good place to take up that goal in the twenty-first century.

A Peck of Dirt

"Mama, she's eating dirt again."

That would be my brother's voice, calling out to Mama, who is only a few yards away. We are outside. She is inside, hearing this panicked cry from the little dirt policeman through the kitchen window as she prepares our midday meal.

That's how I visualize it. I have no memories of those times when Mama dragged me inside and washed my mouth out. I only remember being teased about this early habit, my mother recounting the multiple times that she heard "Mama, she's eating dirt again," how she had to act fast before I swallowed a handful of earth along with whatever might have been living in it.

Hearing about those times, I felt disgust and shame over having been a little dirt eater during my first years as an earthling. I reformed, but sometimes after a rain, when the thick, musky emanations of wet earth came at me in tantalizing waves, the urge returned. Those times, I ate dirt vapors through my nose.

* * *

"Fresh water." The phrase conjures the look and feel of cool, crystalline water, but for the purpose of classifying fish, "fresh water" means "not-salt-water."

Summers, we escaped our New Orleans home to spend time on my grandparents' farm in Opelousas. There, we enjoyed the varieties of fresh water fish caught in the murky lakes, ponds, bayous, and even ditches and canals of the southwest Louisiana prairie. The Fish Man was a regular sight on meatless Fridays. Midmorning, his hulking black sedan, a 1950-something Ford or Chevy, would turn off Highway 190 onto the gravel road where my grandparents lived, blasting the horn and going so fast that a dust cloud chased the car down the road. The need to flag down The Fish Man gave the children a legitimate reason to run and scream, which we did, arms flailing.

He sold fish out of the trunk of his big car. Bream and sac-à-lait were the most prized fish of Prairie Cajuns. But by the time the traveling fishmonger reached my grandparents' road, he often had only the varieties that some people called "trash fish"—gaspergou (nicknamed "gou"), buffalo, alligator gar, and choupique (pronounced SHOE-pick). My stoic family ate, and mostly enjoyed, whatever fish they could get, but I remember some quiet complaints about the choupique. It tasted like mud, the adults said. In fact, its Choctaw name—*shupik*[81]—means mudfish, and it carries a quality called *geosmin,* which is Greek for "smells like dirt."[82] The critter delivered on these promises.

When choupique find themselves in a stagnating body of water depleted of oxygen, they surface and suck air directly into an organ called a swim bladder, using it like a lung. They can live in mud for several days when drought turns ponds into muck, and people sometimes fish for them with a shovel instead of a fishing pole. Choupique love to snack on crawfish, crustaceans known as mudbugs because of their burrowing habits.

Choupique fossils have turned up on four continents.[83] The species has outlived the rest of its family and is now the only surviving member of *Amiidae,* a fish group that originated 180 million years ago.[84] Crawfish fossils date back 150 million years,[85] so the two mud buddies have been in this abusive relationship for eons.

Mud on mud, in mud, with a side of mud. That's a choupique. I loved choupique. That fish was Mother Earth's way of providing me with a socially acceptable way to eat dirt. Dirt, rolled in cornmeal, seasoned with salt and Black pepper, deep-fried in a cast iron skillet, dabbed in ketchup—*heaven.*

* * *

In the 1980s, I was friends with several Afrocentric artists. Many of them wore clothing made of African prints and decorated their homes with fabric drapings and wall hangings. I was drawn to a particular variety of cloth for its simple lines and geometric shapes, repeated patterns of white designs on dark backgrounds.

"It's called mudcloth," my friend Jean told me. "African women weave the cotton cloth, make these designs on it, and then bury the cloth in a certain type of mud." Over a long period of time, she told me, the earth completes the artist's work, darkening areas around the pre-drawn lines so that they stand out in contrast. I was fascinated by the concept of a cooperative effort in which the artist was equal partner to the earth. Here was mud I could eat with my eyes.

I collected mudcloth things: wall hangings, a dress, a hat and coat, a leather-trimmed portfolio, throw pillows. I taught myself clay art and used mudcloth motifs for jewelry and pottery, always mindful of those African women whose designs I tried to replicate.

That was BGE, Before the Google Era. At the dawn of the twenty-first century, I set out to write a meditation on the making of mudcloth, and my research turned up a whole different story about the process. My friend had it all wrong. The cloth is not buried in the earth in mudbug territory. Instead, the women dig up iron-rich mud and leave it to ferment in clay jars for a year. They then apply the mud to the fabric with a brush or a stick with a frayed end, carefully outlining their drawn designs. The people of Mali, where the art originated, call it *bogolan*, meaning "earthcloth."[86]

Though the process is less poetic than I'd been led to believe, I remain a lover of mudcloth. Its making is an act of co-creation, with Mother Earth supplying the raw materials and with water, time, and sunlight playing passive but vital parts in the continuation of an ancient art. And yet, as compelling as the true process sounds, I prefer my friend's erroneous mythos. Despite my new knowledge, I still visualize the hand-woven cloth, with handmade designs, transforming as it rests in the arms of Mother Mud.

* * *

In 1947, an article appeared in *Social Forces* entitled "Notes on Clay and Starch Eating Among Negroes in a Southern Urban Community." At the time it was published, I was a one-year-old Negro in a Southern urban community. The article examines a North Carolina study in which a number of African American women reported digging up and eating a certain type of dirt "without embarrassment." The practice was widespread, with some women eating dirt as a regular habit and some only to satisfy pregnancy cravings. It had to be "good dirt," they said, meaning clay gathered only from certain sites.[87]

While people use the words "dirt" and "clay" interchangeably, the substances are different. Dirt is a mixture of weathered rock, sand, clay, and organic material like decayed leaves. Clay is just weathered rock.

Many articles and studies have looked at dirt-eating habits of Southern African American women. In a 1975 study, a University of Mississippi medical anthropologist found that the women he interviewed preferred hill dirt for its clay content and avoided what they called "gumbo dirt"—dark earth from flat areas that collect moisture. Some ate their clay straight, while others baked it and seasoned it with vinegar and salt.[88] An archeologist interviewed women in the American South in 2004. Many of them ate clay while they were pregnant, believing that it "helped to prevent vomiting, helped babies to thrive, cured swollen legs, and ensured beautiful children."[89]

Dirt-eating has a history and a name. It's called geophagy, from the Greek *gē*, meaning "earth" or "goddess of the earth," and *phagein*, meaning "eat." Geophagy has been practiced around the world since ancient times. Hippocrates, the father of Western medicine, recommended eating dirt for certain illnesses.[90] Native Americans mixed earth into potatoes, baked it into their breads along with corn, and used powdered rock for medicinal purposes. In Africa, the consumption of clay for spiritual and medicinal purposes was widespread.[91] German quarry workers ate a type of clay they called "stone butter," and some Aboriginal Australians ate white clay as a digestive aid and to treat hookworm infection. These practices continue in many cultures across the world.

Plantation owners in the antebellum American South and the West Indies were alarmed by the dirt-eating habit of enslaved Africans and tried to put a stop to it. They believed eating dirt was the slaves' way of making themselves too sick to work or even an attempt to commit suicide. Slave owners were so convinced of the detrimental effects of dirt-eating that they fitted the slaves with face masks to prevent the practice or confined them in stocks as punishment. Physicians of the time considered dirt-eating a malady, calling it *Cachexia Africana*.[92] A researcher who reviewed these theories writes that there is much evidence that the Africans were driven by "a desire to ease their hunger or to satisfy an even more deep-seated appetite."[93] Physicians apparently satisfied themselves with an invented medical diagnosis, rather than admit to an underlying basis for the cravings of human beings living under brutal bondage in a strange land.

Despite the efforts of slaveholders and the opinions of doctors, geophagy continued, and according to some, it spread to rural whites.[94] Southern white geophagists were called "clay eaters." A researcher who reviewed documents going back to 1862 writes that they were considered "the most degraded of the 'poor white trash' [living] in the barren and sandy areas of the southeastern [. . .] and the Gulf states." In South Carolina, they were known as "sandlappers," and an antebellum schoolteacher in Georgia described them as "[i]gnorant, dirty, shiftless, uncouth[,] morally degraded, [and] thoroughly despised." Rather than digging the clay from the ground, the clay eaters sometimes chiseled it out of the packed earth that held their log cabins and hearths together.[95] A contemporary writer tells of a family of clay eaters in Alabama who ate so much earthen grouting from their home's hearth that it threatened collapse.[96]

Cannibalizing one's hearth and home seems most odd, but the practice dates back to a time well before the clay eaters and sandlappers were labeled. Archeologists describe a similar practice in other parts of the world going back to the Paleolithic Era. Certain pockmarks on stone are called cupmarks, rounded indentations about one to two inches in diameter, little excavations made in rocks and boulders by repeatedly pounding one spot with a hard stone.

Some archeologists call them artifacts of geophagy. The process of making a cupmark resulted in about a tablespoon of powdered rock that was ingested for medicinal or spiritual purposes. Cupmarks are found on the Easter Island heads, the Olmec heads in Mexico, and on the sides of houses in parts of Africa. In Germany, Sweden, France, and Switzerland, cupmarks have been pounded into the brick and mortar of churches, both on the insides and outsides of the buildings. An archeologist reported that people were still cupmarking the walls of European churches in the 1880s.[97]

Contemporary geophagists in the state of Georgia prize white clay, called kaolin, which consists of weathered granite, essentially the same substance that the cupmarkers rendered by pulverizing rock. Excavating a Georgia site, archeologists discovered a surprising number of cupmarks near Stone Mountain.[98] It could be that the much maligned clay eaters and sandlappers were heirs to cupmarkers of the distant past.

* * *

My mother used to say, "You have to eat a peck of dirt before you die." Since she so conscientiously disrupted my early attempts to meet that quota, I assumed she was referring to the semi-accidental ingestion of earth. As kids, when we dropped a piece of food on the floor or the ground, if it was something we really hated to forfeit, we'd pick it up, make the sign of cross over it, recite the incantation—"devil kissed it, God made it"—thus pulling divine rank, and then eat the pretend-cleansed food. Why waste a good cookie, potato chip, or orange wedge?

On my grandparents' farm, we ate peaches, plums, pears, and figs right off the trees, veil of dust and all. We picked up pecans from the ground, cracked them open, and ate the flesh with our dirty hands. When our visits to the farm coincided with a harvest, we sampled everything as we reaped. My uncle always had a pocket knife on him, and as soon as the first white potato or yam was unearthed, he'd brush off the loose dirt, pare the tuber, and cut slices for everyone to have a taste.

My grandparents created a temporary earthen vessel to make their filé—powdered sassafras used to flavor and thicken gumbo. Their method contributed to the family's dirt intake. They would dig a small hole in the dry earth, line it with a clean rag, and then nestle in some dried sassafras leaves. They pounded the leaves with a fat, rounded stick, turning them into a fine greenish-brownish powder. The chore took effort and time, and it must have resulted in some transfer, the thin membrane of cotton fabric letting in some dirt particles to mix with the filé while allowing the return of some sassafras to the earth. With the task done, the hole-in-the-ground vessel was filled in. Unlike a cupmark, the earthen mortar and pestle left no evidence behind. A new one would be dug the next season.

Like the practice of geophagy, the peck of dirt adage has roots. An Episcopal priest who blogs under the name The Crone had a grandmother who gave out the same peck-of-dirt advice. The Crone has come to see the wisdom in it, noting that getting some dirt germs into the body triggers the production of antibodies. Our obsession with cleanliness means that "today we are only eating a speck, not a peck, of dirt," resulting in weakened immune systems.[99]

"Let Your Kids Get Dirty!" That's the title of an article written by the mother of a three-year-old daughter. "That's what childhood is for—getting dirty. It's good for her," she writes. Her article lists the benefits children derive from playing outside, and especially playing in dirt: lower rates of asthma, eczema, attention disorders, depression, obesity, stress, and blood pressure problems. She calls the absence of such play "nature-deficit disorder."[100]

The purposeful dirtying up of children is rooted in something called the "hygiene hypothesis." A 1989 study of German children found lower rates of asthma and allergies in children living in rural areas.[101] Stopping short of advocating geophagy, proponents of the hygiene hypothesis encouraged families with children to form more intimate relationships with dirt. Dirt may also benefit the mind and mood. Researchers at two universities in England treated mice (depressed individuals, presumably) with bacteria found in soil. The mice responded as if they had been given an antidepressant drug. The researchers theorize that the bacteria found in soil may increase the release of serotonin in the brain. One of the scientists said that the results of the study "leave us wondering if we shouldn't all be spending more time playing in the dirt."[102]

* * *

My friend Ev and I were in my backyard in New Orleans one day. It had rained earlier, and the aroma of rich earth seemed to suffuse every molecule of the air. We were maybe thirteen years old at the time and had been neighbors and close friends for half our lives, but the subject of dirt-eating had never arisen. I don't remember why we were in the yard. Maybe we were hanging laundry, maybe just hanging out.

One of us said, "The dirt smells *sooooo* good." The other agreed.

One of us said, "I used to eat dirt," and the other confessed the same sin.

The conversation went on for a moment, the revelation tightening our already strong bond. And then one of us said, "Let's eat some." Ev is not here to contradict me, so I'll say it was her idea, and I was the weak-willed follower. But in truth, the tempting idea always entered my head when rain created that alluring bouquet. Suddenly, we were in the Garden of Eden and both of us were Eve.

There was a bald spot towards the back of the yard where no grass grew. We rushed over to it, bent down, scooped a nice portion of soft, damp black earth with our fingers, and stuffed it into our mouths. Words are inadequate to capture the experience. Or, to be more accurate, we lost our ability to speak words and resorted to sound effects like "*PA-TOO-EE!*" and other unspellable noises. We ran for the nearest water source to wash out our mouths, projectile spitting at the earth as we hustled into the garage where there was a faucet.

We were cured. We agreed that this was the dumbest thing we had ever done in our lives. Since that day, I have been satisfied to take in the aroma of wet dirt without being seized by the desire to go all geophagistic.

Decades later, food writer Anne Zimmerman had a sort of parallel experience, but way more dignified than that of Ev and me. Zimmerman reluctantly accepted an invitation to a dirt tasting in San Francisco, something billed as Taste of Place, an installation art event. This dirt tasting stopped short of actually eating dirt, relying on other senses.

Six people gathered at the artist's studio and were handed wine glasses that contained dirt from nearby farms—dirty dirt that included naturally occurring rock, silt, twigs, and bugs. The host mixed a little water into each glass of dirt, making brown mud. She then asked her guests to smell the mud and describe its bouquet.

Zimmerman compared the stirring, swirling, and sniffing of mud to wine tasting, and the group responded with descriptors like "salty, silty, minerally, wet, earthy, and green."

Next, the artist had them eat collard green leaves from plants that had been grown at the farm from which the dirt had been collected. Zimmerman was "startled" to find that "the greens tasted how the dirt smelled, dark and earthy and vegetal." The guests tasted other foods, including herbs, eggs, and cheese, after sniffing the soils from the farms that produced them.

They made similar connections between food and soil. Zimmerman was won over, graduating from reluctant participant to aficionado, "fervently contemplating the aroma profile of the earth."[103] The other participants "were visibly invigorated" by the experience, she writes. One person actually tasted the dirt, an impulsive act, I would guess, and one that Ev and I could certainly have related to. But I wonder if that person ran off spitting dirt and searching for a palate cleanser? The writer doesn't say.

The artist behind the project is Laura Parker. She describes dirt sniffing in terms that could be mistaken for wine-tasting pronouncements: "The nose is both flinty and grassy with finesse and subtlety. [. . .] An underlying presence of cream opens up to hints of citrus and spice."[104] At first glance, Parker's concept of dirt-based installation art might appear gimmicky, but it is based on her commitment to fostering consumer awareness of how our food is produced. Her interest is from the ground up, and it began in her childhood, when she witnessed the farmers in her family tasting dirt to determine acid/alkaline balance before planting season.

The phenomenon that Zimmerman described, the collard greens tasting like the dirt smelled, is called synesthesia, "a sensation produced in one modality when a stimulus is applied to another modality."[105] Except for my last dirt-tasting experience, which was wretched and traumatic, I don't have any memory of the taste of dirt. And yet, as a child, I knew that choupique tasted like dirt. It must be that I was tasting through my nose somehow. The Urban Dictionary offers a new word for the particular experience of synesthesia in which one thing tastes like another thing smells. The word is "smaste," as in "choupique smastes like dirt."[106] *Aha!*

* * *

Why do people eat dirt? One researcher has called geophagistic practitioners victims and addicts who indulge in a "filthy and degrading habit," a "malady" that presents "a major medical problem" in the South. He attributed the practice to a desire to quiet hunger pains, the pleasure of chewing, or the need for social approval.[107]

Some researchers and journalists have asked people who actually eat clay or dirt what they get out of it:

> "It melts in your mouth like chocolate. [. . .] The good stuff is real smooth. [. . .] It's just like a piece of candy."

> "Every time I get pregnant, I get a craving—I have to eat it."

> "If I could get just one little bitty piece, that would stop the craving. [. . .] It has a fresh, natural-feeling taste, like the rain or something."

> "The old drunks, they used to get drunk and put it [clay] in water and drink it, then go to work. The old-timers and people in Louisiana and Mississippi—they just love to eat that Mississippi mud."[108]

> "I feel awful, just about crazy when I can't get clay."[109]

> From a former geophagist: "[. . .] [T]here are times when I really miss it [. . .] I wish I had some dirt right now."[110]

Southern writer Roy Blount defends geophagists in an essay called "I Don't Eat Dirt Personally," in which he describes being a dinner guest in a "chic salon" in New York. Someone asked him about the dirt-eating habits of Southerners. "'Hell, yes,' he replied, 'we eat dirt. And if you never ate any blackened red dirt, you don't know what's good. I understand you people up here eat raw fish.'"[111]

* * *

A 1984 *New York Times* article predicted the demise of geophagy in the South. The researcher quoted in the article had interviewed some Mississippi families who frequently mailed local dirt to relatives who had moved North. Still, he believed the practice of dirt eating to be "clearly on the wane," as some reformed geophagists told him they had grown uncomfortable with the stigma it carried.[112] Three decades after that prediction, far from waning, the practice has become more mainstream and gained culinary and scientific respect.

In May of 2014, David Letterman interviewed actress Shailene Woodley, then twenty-two. "Clay is one of my favorites," she said, "because if you look at indigenous cultures around the world, people are eating clay almost daily [to bind] [. . .] toxins and heavy metals and help you excrete those materials."

Letterman, playfully incredulous, asked Woodley, "Have you heard of Metamucil?"[113]

A geography professor from a Texas university visited a soul food restaurant in Chicago, a frequent stop for tour buses. There, he witnessed Asian tourists enjoying traditional Southern foods: chitlins, greens, and pan-fried Mississippi clay seasoned with vinegar and pepper.[114]

The National Institutes of Health studied the use of clay in curing infections. In lab tests, one type of clay killed "*Staphylococcus aureus*, Methicillin-resistant *Staphylococcus aureus* (MRSA), penicillin resistant *Staphylococcus aureus* (PRSA), and pathogenic *Escherichia coli* (*E. coli*)."[115] An article published in 2000 reported on eating clay as a means of alleviating morning sickness.[116] A medical doctor, nutrition expert at the Yale School of Medicine, and medical contributor to ABC News reported in 2005 that "[i]t is possible that the binding effect of clay would cause it to absorb toxins."[117] In a book published in 2004, an archaeologist who looked at geophagy in different cultures around the world takes a basic biological view of the question of why: "Like other animals, humans appear to instinctively know to ingest clay and rock powder for stomach problems."[118]

Markets have long since taken a side in the debate over the risks and benefits of geophagy. In 1936, while researchers were still branding clay eaters with labels, a Tennessee-based company introduced Kaopectate, a medication for stomach distress that is named for its original content: kaolin and pectin.[119]

Kaolin deposits formed millions of years ago in what became the Southern states. Today, in addition to its use a stomach soother, it is used in the manufacture of cosmetics, paper, and china, among other things, with mining profits running into the billions.[120]

Chuck Reece, editor of the newsletter The Bitter Southerner, has written about geophagy. The South's large kaolin deposit falls along the Black belt, creating an intersection of geography, culture, and history. "Upwards of one million enslaved Africans were brought to work on the area's plantations [. . .] many from West Africa, where geophagy was historically a part of the culture."[121]

In the early 1930s, the boll weevil devastated cotton crops in the South. The Great Depression and severe drought made a bad situation even worse for farmers,[122] but their hardship presented opportunity for others. Reece writes: "White kaolin barons paid pittances for the mineral rights to land owned by countless African American farm families along the fall line."[123]

* * *

In the twenty-first century, one can eat fried clay in a Midwestern soul food restaurant, see it validated as a health food by a new generation, and read about it as the subject of legitimate scientific inquiry. It is no wonder that there's a budding self-help market for the clay craver and the clay curious. Websites, Facebook pages, and Yahoo groups market directly to consumers and offer advice for applying clay to the body or adding it to a smoothie.[124] We may be catching up to the ancients.

In light of these discoveries, I am thinking of resuming my dirt consumption. A peck is equal to eight quarts, I have learned—a considerable amount. I'm sure I'm a few quarts low. Very soon, when I hear my brother's voice in my head warning Mama that *she's eating dirt again*, I'll be able to answer, "Yes, I am. I ordered it from MississippiMiracleClay.com."

Dueling With Martin

Martin Guillory's Civil War sword hung on the wood-paneled den wall of my aunt's camelback house in New Orleans. Generations eyed it with wonder. The rust-encrusted sword was long and curved, with a metal half-circle hand guard and tapered tip, blunt from age. We had roots that we could touch because of this heavy evidence he left behind. The ancestral sword had a presence about it that seemed to convey something of the man as if through osmosis, as if touching, or simply staring at, his sword told his story. His grandchildren, my mother's generation, called him Pere-Pere Martin, and described him as brown-skinned and not very tall. He was married three times, made his wives and children call him Mr. Guillory, fathered so many sons that he ran out of boys' names and ended up calling two of them Martin and two of them John. My grandfather was one of the Johns.

Before the sword came to dwell at my aunt's house in New Orleans, before I was born, it hung on a wall in my grandparents' home in Opelousas, Louisiana. My cousin Mary remembers the exact spot it occupied and tells me that she was afraid of it when she was a child. Joseph and John Junior, her young uncles, told her that Pere-Pere Martin had cut off several men's heads with the sword and that their ghosts roamed the house at night, seeking revenge. She was certain that the dark rust that penetrated the metal was the ancient blood of dead men, and she exerted a lot of prayerful energy trying to keep the angry ghosts out of her room at night.

I was taken captive by the sword's mystery—its connection to the past. History was the real ghost. I got older, learned what the Civil War had been about, and began to ask questions about Pere-Pere Martin. I don't recall whose nerves I was getting on the day that I got an answer I couldn't process, but some adult family member told me that Pere-Pere

Martin had fought on the side of the Confederacy. I was stunned into silence. The Confederacy. It was said softly, with dull delivery, as if this fact was known to all the world except me. The word exploded inside my head, demanding explanation. A Black Confederate! God in heaven—how could that be?

I had thought of Pere-Pere Martin as a hero, a fighter for freedom. To be told that he was on the other side of freedom was an impossible idea to take in. The thought that I might have come from such tainted roots drove me to become a nuisance. "How did Pere-Pere Martin end up on the wrong side of the Civil War?" I wanted to know. No one had a good answer. An elder told me that "they" had the power to force men to serve. I tried to understand this—the undesignated all-powerful "they" imposed their will on people who were not allowed to say no. "Was Pere-Pere Martin a slave?" I asked. Nobody knew, or possibly no one admitted to knowing. The people who could have told me the answer were all long dead.

But whether or not he was enslaved, there were more questions to be considered in trying to bounce back from this shock. If an enslaved man were suddenly armed, why would he fight to preserve slavery when he could choose to fight to end it? And, if he was of the *gens de colour libres*, the free people of color, I would still ask why he would side with the slave-owning class. What would he have to gain by it? And besides, why would a Confederate general arm any Black man, enslaved or free, when the Black man might just turn around and slice off the head of the very Confederate who armed him with that sword?

There was no satisfactory answer to the question of why a Black man would fight to preserve slavery, and yet it had happened, and I felt implicated. I was a freak of history. This great grandfather whom I had never known had done a terrible disservice to his African American heirs, casting us all into a strange rebel universe where we didn't belong. I tried hard but couldn't find a way to get us out of it. I could only come back again and again to place blame on Pere-Pere Martin, the one who had put us here. Then what? What could I do with this resentment, having no living target to aim it at?

The adults knew just how to bring my investigation to a close. "He deserted," they told me. This was one fact they all agreed on. My mother's generation remembered the stories Pere-Pere Martin told them about how he and other deserters made their way back to their hometowns on foot from a long way off, with no food or water, eating dead animals they found along the way and drinking rain water that collected in the deep hoof prints of horses.

> *This was all we had to redeem you, Pere-Pere—you deserted the Confederacy. You turned your back on the ignoble cause. This would have to be enough.*

I hid my awareness of our Confederate heritage well under the surface and told very few people about it. The sword became tinged with an embarrassment of my own creation, stuck there along with the rust that held it together. Life went on for the rebel Black Guillorys. It was odd, though, sitting around the table, looking into the faces of Martin's descendants—his children and his grandchildren and his great grandchildren, Confederate descendants all. I tried to see something in their eyes that might tell me how to accept this unwanted label. No one dwelled on it; they seemed to just accept it, and no one wanted to talk about it. I had to go along with that.

When I met Ted, who would become my husband, I told him about my Confederate ancestry, not wanting to take the chance that he might find out later and denounce and divorce me as a Black daughter of the Confederacy. What if we had children together someday? That would make Ted the father of little African American Confederates. He had a right to know. I made my confession, emphasizing the part about the desertion, telling it the way I had once heard my uncle phrase it: "He deserted and so they lost." Giving our ancestor credit for the Emancipation was the only part of the story I could ever find humor in.

I expected to see an expression of shock on Ted's face, but nothing registered there. He finally hunched his shoulders and said something like, "Nobody's perfect." A feeling of complete amnesty washed over me.

Years after I graduated from college, I saw a small ad in a journal announcing the availability of graduate school scholarships for descendants of Confederate soldiers—a kind of affirmative action program for the sons and daughters of the Confederacy. I considered applying, but mainly just to freak people out.

I showed the ad to Ted. He said, "Yeah, you should do it. Go for it! Make them turn you down and tell you why!"

But I was in no position to go to school at the time, and I also had to take into account the fact that I would be exposing my Black Confederate underside to the world. And then there was the detail that I had no proof of my Confederate lineage except for family stories and a rusty sword on the wall of my aunt's den. There was the little technicality of the desertion, too.

I told my mother about the idea of applying for this Confederate financial aid, thinking she would find it funny. I was in the middle of saying something about Pere-Pere Martin the Confederate when she looked at me in disbelief.

"He was not a Confederate. Where did you get that idea?" she asked.

"I don't know. . . . Someone told me. . . ."

"No," she said, "Pere-Pere Martin would have been in the Union Army. It wouldn't make no sense for him to be a Confederate."

"But y'all said . . . I know y'all told me he was a Confederate."

"What 'y'all'? Not me. I never told you that."

"But the sword, the stories about him deserting . . ."

"The sword is real, and yes, he was a deserter, but I don't know who told you he was a Confederate. That wouldn't make no sense."

Could all those years of secrecy and embarrassment have been pointless? What was the truth, and could I ever know it? Mama had said, "That wouldn't make no sense," relying on history and logic. She had no evidence, yet she was unwilling to consider any alternative to her ideas about Pere-Pere Martin's military affiliation, and I had no grounds to disagree with her.

But oddly, I wasn't able to renounce my Confederate heritage on the spot that night. I had grown up with it; it had been metabolized and become part of me—maybe not a desirable part, but familiar flesh like an ugly mole that, though you might keep it hidden, the thought of lancing makes you flinch.

Martin and I gradually joined the Union side. Mama was right; Confederate affiliation was unthinkable. But accepting my mother's logic meant that I had to decipher Martin all over again from scratch. If he was a Union soldier, then there was the desertion to rethink. This was the bothersome thing that had kept me wavering for a time before I could fully switch sides. The desertion. My family had managed to attribute some honor to that act, but now its whole character changed as Martin went from gray to blue. He was on the Union side, the right side, the *as-he-died-to-make-men-holy-let-us-die-to-make-men-free* side—but he deserted!

> *Oh, Martin, you just couldn't get it right, could you? Well, at least we could say that you were a survivor. Yes, that would have to do. A survivor with a big sword.*

Potential scholarship qualification evaporated, illegitimate and insincere though it may have been, I stashed the confusing ghost of Pere-Pere Martin way in the back of my mind again. Except for my efforts to place him and his three wives and all of the Martins and Johns in our family history, I hardly thought of him.

Decades passed. One night, my fourth cousin John, a great-great grandson of Pere-Pere Martin, called me from his home in Memphis. He had heard that I was attempting to piece together the fractured limbs of the Guillory family tree. He asked me what had become of Martin's sword, and I told him that our cousin Dee had inherited the job of sword-keeper from her grandmother.

John seemed hesitant in asking his next question: "Did anyone ever tell you that Martin was a Confederate soldier in the Civil War?"

> *Oh no, Martin! Are you going to make me switch sides again? I'm getting very tired of you, Pere-Pere.*

But then, before I could finish venting my confusion, Cousin John told me that the two disparate accounts could both be correct: Martin Guillory had most likely been both a Confederate soldier and a Union soldier.

The sword had always fascinated John. He questioned Martin Guillory's Confederate allegiance and sought out more information about the "colored regiments" of the Civil War. John learned that Martin Guillory was a member of the Louisiana Native Guards, the Black arm of Louisiana's State Militia. They were a ceremonial presence, marching in parades, wearing uniforms, and carrying swords. As part of the state militia, they were counted as Confederates, but they soon found that they were on the wrong side.

I know very little about Martin Guillory, but I learned recently that he was born of an enslaved mother and a free father, and at some point he was emancipated. He joined the Louisiana Native Guards as a free man of color at the beginning of the Civil War. Why? It seems like an irrational act. But looking at the story of another man, one whose path may have paralleled Martin's, I have gained a sense of how this all came about.

André Cailloux, like Martin, was born into slavery. He was emancipated in 1846 at age twenty-one, and while Martin became a farmer in rural Louisiana, New Orleanian Cailloux became a shopkeeper, boxer, horseman, homeowner, husband, and father. He is remembered as being a handsome man, well liked and trustworthy, who proudly called himself "the Blackest man in New Orleans." In 1860, Cailloux joined the Friends of Order, a benevolent society of New Orleans free people of color, and was elected its secretary. The start of the Civil War meant that community organizations were expected to join the state militia. People of color had fought in America's wars since the Revolution, and the expectation of service applied to them as well as to white citizens. Cailloux's Friends of Order became the Order Company in the Louisiana Native Guards. He enlisted free and enslaved men for his company and served as their captain.[125]

Within a few months of the creation of the Native Guards, Louisiana reorganized its militia, making it open to white males only. According to historian Joseph Logsdon, "The Confederates were nervous about the presence of Black troops [. . .] didn't know what was on their minds. People living in a slave society have constant fears of a revolt." The Native Guardsmen were also ready to change sides, as their white commanders were only interested in using them as propaganda, as evidence that Blacks were in favor of the Southern status quo.[126]

Reading about the Native Guards, I encountered a phrase many times, that expression that goes "when New Orleans fell," referring to the point at which New Orleans was overtaken and held by the Union army. Point of view counts for something. I doubt that the Guardsmen saw this as a fall. It was an opportunity. It meant that the Union army was in charge of Louisiana's largest city. Native Guardsmen and runaway slaves began offering their services to the Union Army in New Orleans. General Benjamin Butler was the Union commander there.

He asked Native Guardsmen who volunteered to serve in the Union Army why they had joined Louisiana's militia when it was becoming part of the Confederate army. The men told Butler "they had organized the unit because they wanted to tamp down any suspicion of Black disloyalty during the war hysteria of the spring of 1861."[127]

Historian Donald R. Shaffer writes that the long obscure story of the Native Guards has recently "gained notoriety as extreme Southern partisans have pointed to it as evidence that [. . .] African-Americans fought for the Confederacy, a contention that modern Civil War scholars [including Shaffer] firmly reject."[128] Neo-Confederates, anxious to prove the existence of Black support for their side, have gone so far as to doctor a photograph of Native Guardsmen, cropping out their uniformed white Union officer and passing the picture off as an all-Black Confederate contingent.[129] According to curators and historians, there are nine known photographs of Black men wearing Confederate uniforms. Four of them are known to be images of men owned by Confederate officers who brought them onto the battlefield as personal servants. One photo depicts a man who in reality was an agent for the Union cause. Little is known about the other four men.[130]

Along with free men of color who wished to join the Union cause, runaway slaves began streaming into New Orleans, seeking Union protection. One officer described them as "old and young, little ones and all [. . .] suffering from exposure, and uncertainty, some loaded with chains and barbarous irons; some bleeding with birdshot wounds [or] deeply scored with lashes."[131] For Black men offering military service, joining the Union side was not a simple matter of just showing up in New Orleans. General Butler at first refused to enlist Black men in the military. He lacked confidence in their ability to fight, and he feared arming them with guns, not knowing what they might do with those guns.[132] When an officer proposed raising a Black Union regiment, Butler wrote in a letter that the man "has gone crazy."[133]

The Black people seeking refuge in the Union-held area were encamped under armed guard and put to work as laborers and servants for the white Union soldiers and officers. Butler reportedly said that "he used the labor of the negroes as he would that of a horse or mule," and he ordered his soldiers "to shoot any Negro who tried to leave [the camps] without a pass."[134]

In the interest of producing food crops for the army and the surrounding community, he returned many runaways to plantations, even though the practice was prohibited by an article of war. He assigned Union soldiers to act as plantation overseers. A New Orleans official condemned this arrangement, charging Butler with "reestablishing slavery."[135]

General Butler's refusal to enlist the guardsmen and former slaves meant that they had to live without means in the swampy, disease-laden areas around New Orleans, waiting to serve the Union. Many of them died from disease, exposure, or starvation.[136] But then things changed, and General Butler had to reassess. Although he was a military man on the Union side, he had hoped to win back the loyalty of the slave owners by leaving their system intact. In July of 1862, President Lincoln's early draft of the Emancipation Proclamation made it clear that the system was doomed. At the same time, Butler was also aware of the likelihood that the Confederates would attempt to retake New Orleans. With no white reinforcements en route, he decided to "call on Africa."[137]

September 27, 1862, the 1st Regiment of the Louisiana Native Guards became the first Black regiment allowed into the Union Army. The 2nd and 3rd Regiments were formed soon afterward. The Union muster roll listed André Cailloux as a captain and Martin Guillory as a sergeant.[138] These developments made for some very confused record-keeping. The National Archives names Martin Guillory and André Cailloux as belonging to the 1st Regiment, Native Guards, Louisiana Militia on the side of the Confederacy. The same archive also lists Cailloux as a captain in the Union army.[139]

In official records, Pere-Pere Martin, you and your fellow guardsmen are engaged in a Civil War duel with yourselves.

Once mustered in, gaining the respect of the Union side was a battle in itself for the Black soldiers. They faced racial prejudice, including denial of pay and promotion.[140] Black commissioned officers were demoted because "white officers objected to having to salute or otherwise recognize Black peers."[141] White troops disrespected the Black men and refused to drill alongside them.[142] A guardsman wrote his mother, "Nobody really desires our success."[143]

General Butler was replaced by Major General Nathaniel P. Banks, who drove most of the remaining commissioned Black officers out of the service and replaced them with white men. Although the Black soldiers pleaded for combat duty, General Banks assigned them to labor details like digging trenches, chopping wood, building earthenworks, and guarding prisoners.[144] A writer of the time said that the Union's "prejudice and opposition against the use of colored troops was so strong that the war was half finished before they were organized to any extent."[145]

The Battle of Port Hudson was a turning point. Banks at last agreed to battle-test the men, ordering two Native Guards regiments, the 1st and 3rd, to participate in an attack on a Confederate bastion at Port Hudson, Louisiana, along with some thirty thousand white union troops. The objective was to gain control of the Mississippi River. I don't know whether my great-grandfather was there at the famous battle. Gary Hardy's genealogy project has a partial list of Union soldiers who fought at Port Hudson. Captain André Cailloux, one of the few Black commissioned officers who remained after Major General Banks's purge, and who headed a company in Martin Guillory's regiment, is on the list. Martin Guillory's name does not appear. But, according to Hardy, no comprehensive list exists. He compiled his relatively short roster from various sources, including books, letters, and old newspaper articles, and he continues to add names as he uncovers them.[146]

Before the battle commenced, onlookers described the two Black regiments filing through the town as "a fine lot of men [. . .] form[ing] a beautiful line[. T]hey came on in splendid form, bayonets glistening like silver in the bright [. . .] sun, uniforms spick and clean."[147] On May 27, 1863, Captain Cailloux and his men stormed the heavily armed and fortified Confederate bastion at "double-quick pace." Their objective—a hilltop fortress that rose high above the land—lay beyond a wide-open field. Over several days, Cailloux led charge after charge, shouting orders in French and English, "his sword uplifted [. . .] his face the color of the sulfurous smoke that enveloped him and his followers."[148] Confederate landmines, rifles, cannons, and howitzers assailed them from every angle. One Confederate soldier described the barrage as a "volcano of shot and shell."[149] Cailloux was badly wounded by cannon fire that left one of his arms "dangling uselessly by his side." And still he charged, until at last he was killed by Confederate artillery.[150]

Black Union soldiers fought on the left side of the Port Hudson battlefield, while white Union soldiers engaged the enemy a distance away on the right side. After several charges, hundreds of Black and white Union dead and wounded lay on the field, and Major General Banks requested a truce to tend to them. But the prejudice against Black soldiers extended even to the bloody battlefield. A Confederate soldier who witnessed the truce wrote, "The enemy have buried all their white men and left the negroes to melt in the sun."[151] Surviving guardsmen made attempts to rescue the wounded, but each time they did so, they were fired on. When the Confederate soldiers grew sick of the stench of rotting flesh, their commander asked Banks for a truce so that the Confederates could bury the dead guardsmen. "Banks refused, saying that he had no dead in that area."[152]

Confederate soldiers went out to the field of dead and dying guardsmen to pick their pockets, a practice that a Confederate diarist referred to as a "blackberrying expedition" and a "grim pleasantry." Searching through the pockets of one man, they found "eight dollars in green backs" and papers verifying his military commission as Captain André Cailloux of the Union Army.[153]

Some question the military reasons for the staging of an attack against such a well protected fortress. A contemporary historian writes that "the 1st and 3rd Native Guard Regiments were selected to provide a diversionary attack."[154] A Confederate Port Hudson combatant wrote in his diary, "It was astounding that this negro brigade would assault such a place," and another called the men "poor wretches [who] perished in the fatal trap into which they had been so unwisely driven."[155] One writer called the Native Guards' charge "almost suicidal,"[156] another called it a "killing field,"[157] another called it murder,[158] and several writers refer to the battle as the Port Hudson Massacre.[159]

The human cost was great, but the military objective was not achieved. Of the one thousand guardsmen who went into battle, there were six hundred casualties.[160] The Union commander did not order any further attempts to take the Confederate bastion atop the hill, and the attack turned into a forty-eight-day siege. The Confederates finally surrendered when a defeat upriver meant that they had lost control of the Mississippi

River. It was then that André Cailloux's remains were retrieved from the killing field, forty-three days after his death in battle. He was honored with a hero's funeral in New Orleans.

* * *

Reading about the Battle of Port Hudson, I encountered the words "test" and "trial" many times. Military leaders had long doubted the Black troops' ability and courage to fight, and their performance in battle had answered those doubts. Major General Banks, who showed such contempt for the fallen Black soldiers, announced to the world that the men had passed "[t]he severe test to which they were subjected."[161] The website of the Louisiana State Parks looks back on the participation of the Black troops and calls it a "bold experiment."[162]

With the battle lost, little attention was paid to its military objectives, and commenters in the government, the military, and the press spoke mostly to the racial implications of passing the test. When Banks commended the regiments of the Louisiana Native Guards, he spoke not of what they had accomplished for the cause but of how "the Phalanx won honor for the race it represented."[163] Louisiana Congressman B. F. Flanders said "they fought like devils [and] completely conquered the prejudice of the army against them," calling the new appreciation for the men an unprecedented "turnaround in sentiment."[164] Twenty years after the Battle of Port Hudson, E. Longpie, a surviving Native Guardsman, wrote a letter describing his experiences even as he noted the difficulty of writing with a hand that had suffered wounds in battle. He asked, "What did it avail to hurl a few thousand troops against those impregnable works?" "The men were not iron," he wrote, but more "a subject of test."[165]

William Welles Brown, who wrote of the bravery of Captain Cailloux and the men he led, asked the question, "[H]ad they accomplished anything more than the loss of many of their brave men?" He answered: "Yes: they had. The self-forgetfulness, the undaunted heroism, and the great endurance of the negro, as exhibited that day, created a new chapter in American history for the colored man."[166]

Longpie, contemplating the same question, wrote of the certainty of a dire outcome for all Black soldiers had things gone differently: "Had these two regiments failed, or destiny betrayed their courage, the colored troops would have been universally condemned, and would not have been employed as soldiers, but used as servants, drivers, and laborers, on fortifications, bridges, and ditches."[167]

According to Brown, thirty-five guardsmen were taken prisoner in the aftermath of the battle.[168] They were doomed. Jefferson Davis, president of the Confederacy, had ordered that captured Black soldiers, along with their white officers, were to be executed.[169] Witnesses who lived in the town of Port Hudson reported seeing the bodies of Black Union soldiers hanging from trees in the woods.[170] In a later battle in another state, an officer and twenty of his Black soldiers were captured and hanged.[171] Almost a year after the Battle at Port Hudson, Confederate General Nathan Bedford Forest ordered surrendering Black soldiers at Fort Pillow to be "shot down like dogs."[172] Some three hundred men were killed.[173]

Though historians call the participation of the 1st and 3rd in the Battle of Port Hudson a turning point, the 2nd regiment was battle-tested on a smaller scale the month before. April of 1863 found members of the 2nd Regiment deployed off the coast of Mississippi on Ship Island, where they were charged with digging artillery fortifications in the sand and guarding prisoners. Hearing word of Confederates in the area, the Union commander sent a contingent of guardsmen ashore to engage the enemy. He reported that the men "fought intelligently[,] replying volley with volley while repulsing attack after attack in the streets."[174] The enemy was driven out of Pascagoula within hours.

In her book of poems entitled *Native Guards*, Natasha Trethewey describes what came next. Returning to their waiting ship, the men were surprise-attacked by Confederate soldiers. Being outnumbered and outgunned, they ran for the Union gunboat *Jackson*, which had ferried them ashore earlier that day. White Union sailors aboard the *Jackson* "fired directly at [the Black Union soldiers] and not at the oncoming Confederates."[175] Six of them were killed and several were wounded.

To call these circumstances difficult for the Black soldiers would be a massive understatement. They faced down the enemy before them, yet behind and beside them, deadly prejudice from within their own ranks lay like a coiled snake. Martin Guillory had a reason for calling himself a deserter, but I cannot know the why or the when. Did he fight with his regiment at Port Hudson, or did unbearable circumstances drive him out even before that? Whatever happened, Martin ended up on a long and difficult journey back to his home in Opelousas. He died at the approximate age of ninety-five, probably cursing both the blue and the gray.

* * *

Postbellum. Eventually, the two battered sides of the Civil War merged back into one wounded nation, and all of the soldiers were simply called veterans. Louisiana began granting pensions to Confederate veterans in 1898. My cousin Mary, who so feared the sword when she was a little girl, is the oldest of Martin's great-grandchildren in the lineage of his third wife and the only member of my generation who remembers him. She recalls that in his elder years, he applied repeatedly for a veteran's pension and was denied each time. Apparently he had no choice but to apply as a Confederate, since that remains his official designation in our nation's military archive.

I can imagine how the pension pursuit would have looked: Martin Guillory, elder, on the verge of the new century, too old to farm, approaching the Opelousas courthouse on horseback, or maybe in the wagon he used to carry his cotton to market and his children to Mass, bearing his sword with him for evidence, or maybe for intimidation; then later, into the new century, one of his sons would have chauffeured him in a Ford Model T to the brick buildings of higher authority to file his numerous doomed appeals, his son begging him to *please leave that sword in the car, Mr. Guillory.*

> *Oh, you tenacious, indefatigable drinker of filthy horse-hoof rainwater, you two-hundred-mile walker, you sword-wielding Louisiana Native Guardsman, you deserting Union-joining reb, you would-be Black Confederate pensioner. What nerve! You must have been thrown out of every official building in South Louisiana.*

If Pere-Pere and I could have a talk now, I would tell him . . . *Stop calling yourself a deserter, Pere-Pere Martin! It doesn't become you. You made the best choices for yourself and your people.*

And then I would tell him about my notion to apply for that Confederate scholarship. I'm certain that he would not find the idea funny at all. He would say . . .

> *Mais oui! Go put in your application, cher. Take my sword with you!*

On the Treaty of Paris, the Book of Negroes, and Harry Washington

An eighteenth-century oil painting depicts five men, citizens of the new nation of America. They are garbed in aristocratic frippery: linen breeches, frock coats and waistcoats over white shirts with ruffled cuffs and collars, their legs covered by white knee-high stockings, feet buckled into pointy-toed shoes. The painting's subjects are John Jay, John Adams, Henry Laurens, Benjamin Franklin, and his grandson William Franklin, secretary to the gathering of leaders. Powdered wigs crown the heads of four of the five men. Benjamin Franklin eschews that affectation, choosing a more natural look, and without a frock coat, his white shirtsleeves are exposed. All of them divert their eyes from us except Ben, who pins the viewer with a gentle stare, or perhaps he is looking in our direction but beyond us. Solemn facial expressions befit the import of the occasion—the men are poised to put their John Hancocks to the 1783 Treaty of Paris, recognizing America's independence from Great Britain. At the center of the painting, a half-unfurled parchment scroll representing the document cascades over the edge of a partially completed table.

The founding fathers take up the center and the left side of the painting. The right side is a big messy blotch that looks as if someone has rubbed the wet oil paints away, leaving white canvas mottled with stains, or as if some catastrophe befell the artist, Benjamin West, preventing him from completing the final fourth of the work. Other parts of the canvas have a similar unfulfilled quality. Henry Laurens looks as if he is still materializing, his red frock coat not yet fully formed; William Franklin melts into the off-white parchment laid out before him, poetically appropriate for the scribe; John Adams's breeches and white-stockinged legs appear ghostly. Behind the group of men is an unfinished backdrop; above their heads, something that looks like a set of dark wings hovers.

John Adams, John Jay, and Benjamin Franklin met with British negotiator Richard Oswald over many sessions in Paris in 1782 to thrash out a preliminary version of the peace treaty that would end the Revolutionary War. Thomas Jefferson, drafter of the Declaration of Independence, was to have joined the Americans for the sessions, but matters in the colonies kept him away. Henry Laurens, former president of the Continental Congress, who looks almost ethereal in the painting, was delayed and missed all but the final session. He arrived in Paris on the last day of talks at the lodgings of the British negotiator just in time to amend the treaty. The tardy Laurens would have a profound impact on the aftermath of the Revolutionary War.

* * *

An ocean away from Paris, well before the outcome of the war would be determined, the impassioned rhetoric of natural rights, freedom, and liberty suffused the ethers in the thirteen colonies. The British military was a seasoned force, and for various reasons, many colonists sided with King George III. They were called Loyalists while revolutionaries were known as Patriots. Leading Patriot George Washington compared the plight of colonists to that of enslaved Africans, yet the value he placed on freedom did not extend to them. In 1774, Washington wrote to a friend that "we must assert our rights, or submit to every imposition that can be heap'd upon us; till custom and use, will make us as tame, and abject slaves, as the Blacks we rule over with such arbitrary sway."[176]

In the midst of the contest of ideas, eavesdroppers took note. African cooks, servers, nursemaids all had ears that took in the Patriots' talk of rights and freedoms, but once open hostilities flared, it was the British side that offered them a way of pursuing their own dreams. General Benedict Arnold encouraged the royal governor of Virginia, Lord Dunmore, to invite runaways to join His Majesty's cause and thereby achieve their immediate freedom. The Dunmore Proclamation was issued in 1775, and hundreds of enslaved people escaped plantation bondage and crossed the line not in the name of partisanship, but in the interest of their own freedom. Many volunteered their services to the British military. That same year, George Washington took command of the Continental Army. Although African Americans had fought for the

American cause at Lexington, Concord, and Bunker Hill, Washington barred any further recruitment of Black soldiers. And for those who did fight, there was no promise of freedom.[177]

Dunmore's Proclamation greatly benefitted the cause of freedom for the enslaved, but its basis was not humanitarian. It was a war measure designed to weaken the Patriots' cause by encouraging their workforce to desert them. The Proclamation targeted slaves owned by Patriots and exempted those owned by Loyalists so as not to lose their allegiance.[178] The Patriots were so disturbed by the Proclamation that their complaint made its way into the Declaration of Independence as one of Thomas Jefferson's grievances against King George: "He has excited domestic insurrections amongst us." George Washington, Thomas Jefferson, Patrick Henry, James Madison, and many other prominent Patriots lost slaves to the British after Dunmore issued his proclamation.[179]

Men, women, and children sought British protection and offered their services to the Loyalist side. One of them was named Harry Washington. Born on the Rice Coast in the region of Gambia, he was sold into slavery around 1740 at the approximate age of twenty. He came by his surname when George Washington purchased him in 1763 to become part of an enslaved workforce that numbered 150 during the Revolutionary era.[180] Harry Washington dug drainage canals in Virginia's Great Dismal Swamp and worked at various tasks at Mount Vernon plantation: laborer, horse trainer, and house servant. He had escaped in 1771 but was captured and brought back to Mount Vernon. Learning of the British offer of freedom, he fled the plantation in 1776, met up with a fleet of British ships on the Potomac, and volunteered his services as a Loyalist. While George Washington was commanding the Continental Army in Cambridge, Massachusetts, Harry Washington was being inducted into the king's Ethiopian Regiment (also called the Black Pioneers), a company charged with "Cleaning the Streets & Removing all Nuisances being thrown into the Streets." By 1781, Harry Washington had achieved the rank of corporal and was commanding a company attached to the Royal Artillery Department in Charleston, South Carolina.[181]

* * *

The 1781 Battle of Yorktown set the king's cause back dramatically. Colonial forces captured the British commander Lord Cornwallis. These developments set the Americans on the path to victory, but conditions for a ceasefire had to be worked out between the two sides. Treaty talks began in 1782. The American negotiators held out for independence from Britain as part of a declaration of peace. Warfare between the two sides slacked off following the Battle of Yorktown, but open hostilities continued, and the British military still held and defended some areas in the colonies.

The tardy founding father, Henry Laurens, arrived at the table after the American negotiators' demand for independence from Britain had been ceded, and all parties were prepared to sign the treaty. But Laurens had one more demand to add. At his insistence, an additional provision was agreed to. Article 7 set forth conditions for the withdrawal of the British occupiers. Laurens' addition to that article specified that upon evacuation, the British were prohibited from "carrying away any Negroes or other property of the American Inhabitants." This provision negated the promise of freedom for runaways who had joined the British side and granted slave masters the right to reclaim their property—property like Harry Washington, who was listed in George Washington's inventory as "a man about 40 years old, valuable, a Horseler [horse trainer]."[182]

Despite the fact that this latest provision violated His Majesty's promise of freedom for runaways, British negotiator Richard Oswald did not object. Laurens' words were scribbled in the margin of Article 7, probably by William Franklin the scribe, and the preliminary treaty was signed on November 30, 1782.

During slavery, the expression "sold down the river" was ominous. For an enslaved African, it was the threat and reality of being shipped southward along the Mississippi, being dispatched from a bad place to a worse place, to rice swamps and cane fields where conditions were deadly. The expression has become a metaphor for betrayal of any sort. Both the literal and the figurative meanings apply to the revised Article 7.

John Jay later expressed surprise that Oswald, acting on behalf of the British side, had not objected to the added language.[183] However, both Oswald and Laurens had vested interests in preserving slavery in America. Business dealings that spanned the ocean already tied the two men together in the transatlantic triangular trade between Africa, the Americas, and England.

Oswald, whom Laurens referred to as "my very worthy friend," owned a slave post in Sierra Leone, where captured Africans were held before being shipped to the colonies.[184] Henry Laurens was Oswald's American business agent, handling the sale of his human cargo as slave ships arrived in South Carolina. Before the start of the war, Oswald had been looking to expand his involvement by acquiring land in South Carolina in order to establish his own plantation. He had plans to relocate slaves he already owned in Florida to land owned by his "very worthy friend" Laurens, land that Laurens had agreed to transfer to Oswald for the venture.[185] And beyond that, Laurens was partly indebted to Oswald for his very freedom. Laurens had been captured at sea earlier in the war and imprisoned in the Tower of London in 1781 until Oswald helped secure his bail.[186]

In Benjamin West's oil painting, the part of Laurens' torso where his heart would reside is unpainted, giving him a hollowed-out appearance. Regardless, he was still able to engage in some chest-thumping once he had accomplished his mission. In a letter to John Gervais, his friend and attorney, Laurens took full credit for having "insisted" on the provision concerning the Black Loyalists. Gervais, owner of rice and indigo plantations, lost more runaways to the British than any other plantation owner in the Carolinas, and coincidentally, he owed a great deal of money to British negotiator Oswald for slaves he had purchased on credit before the war began. He would potentially benefit directly from the scribbled addition to Article 7, which would in turn have placed him in a better position to pay off his debt to Oswald. Laurens himself, as Oswald's agent in the slave business and as a slave owner with a large rice plantation, was also positioned to benefit from the provision. Laurens, Oswald, and Gervais—the three back-slapping friends—had a lucrative triangular trade of their own. The late and sole contribution from Laurens to a treaty with implications for the world served to personally benefit some of the principal crafters.

* * *

Word of the Treaty of Paris winged its way across the ocean: "His Britannic Majesty acknowledges the said United States . . . to be free sovereign and independent."[187] However, the revising of Article 7 had turned a quill into a sword that pierced the hearts of the Black Loyalists. The impending British evacuation would leave them without protection, and the measure of their worth would return to that of property, their former owners former no more.

During the war, nearly one hundred thousand enslaved Africans fled from their owners.[188] At the time of the signing of the treaty, approximately twenty thousand of these self-emancipated were living in the major ports still held by the British: New York City, Charleston, South Carolina, Savannah, Georgia, and a small section of Florida.[189] In New York, runaways made up 10 percent of the workforce, holding jobs in construction projects, as nurses and orderlies in hospitals, as laundresses, seamstresses, ship pilots, musicians, racetrack jockeys, cooks, and servants.[190] Harry Washington and other escapees from George Washington's Mount Vernon plantation were among them. No doubt they savored the newfound sense of dignity and self-determination that their freedom brought them.

A Black Loyalist named Boston King, an escapee from a South Carolina plantation, was living as a free man in New York, experiencing what he called "the happiness of liberty, of which I knew nothing before."[191] News of the treaty reached New York, bringing the instant threat of re-enslavement. King wrote in his memoir:

> [...] [P]eace was restored between America and Great Britain, which diffused universal joy among all parties, except us, who had escaped from slavery, and taken refuge in the English army; for a report prevailed at New-York, that all the slaves, in number 2000, were to be delivered up to their masters, altho' some of them had been three or four years among the English. This dreadful rumour filled us all with inexpressible anguish and terror, especially when we saw our old masters coming from Virginia, North-Carolina, and other parts, and seizing upon their slaves in the streets of New-York, or even dragging them out of their beds. Many of the slaves had very cruel masters, so that the thoughts of returning home with them embittered life to us. For some days we lost our appetite for food, and sleep departed from our eyes.[192]

A British officer wrote in his diary that "almost five thousand persons have come into this city [New York] to take possession of their former property."[193] George Washington engaged an army contractor to search for his runaways. Corporal Washington eluded his former master's clutches, though his fortunes would later turn.

In seeking the return of his property, George Washington acted on his instincts as what was euphemistically called "a planter," but in his other job, he was commander in chief of the Continental Army. As such, he was tasked with planning for the transfer of power to the American government, an occasion that would mark the British evacuation deadline in the ports they still held. Washington fully intended to enforce Article 7 on behalf of America's planter class, to capture as many Black people as possible, regardless of their status. On this issue, Washington's counterpart, British Commander in Chief Sir Guy Carleton, faced a dilemma. Black Loyalists besieged Carlton to plead the case for their freedom. They considered themselves to be British subjects and saw the violation of the royal proclamation that promised them freedom as a heinous reversal. Carleton felt that "delivering up Negroes to their former masters [. . .] would be a dishonourable violation of the public faith[,] a flagrant injustice to the slaves [Britain] has manumitted."[194] At his first evacuation negotiation, Carleton informed Washington that in order to speed things along, he had already evacuated approximately six thousand Loyalists, including "a number of Negroes."[195]

In correspondence and face-to-face meetings, Carleton and Washington fought over the fate of the Black Loyalists. Carleton argued that the right of conquest entitled his army to ownership of the slaves "as to any other acquisition or article of prize."[196] But he went further, with a contradictory argument, telling Washington that "the Negroes in question, I have already said, I found free when I arrived at New York, I had therefore no right, as I thought, to prevent their going to any part of the world they thought proper."[197]

If the Black Loyalists were no longer property, their removal would not violate Article 7.[198] Carleton's interpretation subverted the intent of treaty signatories. Washington disputed the reasoning, but the United States Congress, "over vigorous protest from the southern states," instructed him to go along with Carleton's plan to avoid "a renewal of hostilities" between the two countries.[199] Washington had to concede. He lamented in a letter to the governor of Virginia that "the slaves who have absconded from their masters will never be restored to them."[200]

The two commanders reached a compromise. They agreed that Black people who had served with the British military or who had sought protection in British-held areas before the treaty was signed would be allowed to leave with the British military. The evacuation and the transfer of power to the new American government were to be completed by noon on November 25, 1783. Washington wanted documentation of all Black people who were to be carried off so that their former owners could apply for reparations. Carleton complied by creating a board to review each manumission claim and issuing Certificates of Freedom to qualified applicants. He then created *The Book of Negroes*, a roster of names of bearers of certificates.

Washington's agent and other Americans inspected British ships for undocumented runaways—people without certificates of freedom—but they were not authorized to inspect Royal Navy or merchant vessels, ten percent of which were manned by Black seamen. Those ships sailed away uninspected.[201] Patriots searching for their runaways found so many of them in possession of certificates that they charged the British with tipping the scales to favor Black evacuees. George Washington did not retrieve any of his former slaves who resided in New York at that time, and he called the certification process set up by Carleton "little more than a farce."[202]

Harry Washington's name appears in *The Book of Negroes*. He is described as "43, fine fellow. Formerly the property of General Washington; left him 7 years ago." Boston King, who witnessed runaways being carried off by their former masters in New York, is listed in the book as "23, stout fellow. Formerly the property of Richard Waring of Charlestown, South Carolina; left him 4 years ago." In all, the British evacuated three thousand Black people from New York for resettlement in parts of the British Empire.[203] It was July of 1783, eight months after Henry Laurens amended Article 7 of "The Definitive Treaty of Peace between his Britannic Majesty and the United States of America."

Evacuation proceeded in the other British-held ports. In the state of Georgia, the royal commitment to Black Loyalists' freedom had habitually been violated during the war. The British army had treated slaves as spoils of war. They were given to officers as personal servants, used as barter for supplies or as military and farm laborers, plundered by privateers, and sold for profit. And despite the British proclamation promising freedom, runaways trying to join the Loyalist side were often captured by soldiers and returned to their masters for reward. The number of Georgia's slaves was estimated at fifteen thousand before the war. When the evacuation began, that number had been reduced by five thousand, a figure that represented escaped slaves and slaves who were forced to emigrate with their white Loyalist owners.[204] The evacuation of Savannah saw many white Loyalists leaving with their still-enslaved Africans, bound for British-controlled areas where slavery was legal, such as Florida, the Bahamas, Jamaica, and Nova Scotia.[205]

In South Carolina, with evacuation pending, the British military and state legislators busied themselves dividing up the Black people between the two sides. British Major General Alexander Leslie established the Board of Claims and ordered all Blacks, slave and free, to register: "Those certified as the property of white loyalists were to be returned to their owners, the rest would continue to serve as military laborers."[206] Leslie also had to contend with the British officers' practice of claiming slaves as spoils of war, sailing off with them, and selling them outside the colonies, a practice that continued even after the Americans outlawed it. About the Black Loyalists who held the promise of freedom, Leslie was instructed by British Commander Carleton to honor their service by counting them as free persons.

But when evacuation began, there were not enough ships to accommodate all of the Black people who were authorized to leave. They "clamored at the gates of freedom demanding to be counted [among those] entitled to liberty."[207] As the last of the British fleet prepared to set sail, passengers were ferried on longboats to the waiting ships. Those for whom there was no room on the boats were landlocked at the port of Charleston, the very place where Henry Laurens oversaw the disembarkation, warehousing, and auction of an untold number of African captives at the wharf owned by Christopher Gadsden, designer of the "Don't Tread on Me" revolutionary flag. Soldiers held the Black freedom lovers back as the last boats filled up and floated out to the ships. Many became desperate, broke through the line of soldiers, and swam out to the boats. "Clinging to the sides of the longboats, they were not allowed on board, but neither would they let go; in the end, their fingers were chopped off."[208]

The left-behind former slaves almost certainly faced re-enslavement. But for many of those who did evacuate, the quest for freedom did not end with a triumphant sailing off into the sunset. Many Black evacuees landed in British settlements in the Caribbean. Lord Dunmore, who issued the proclamation that led many of them to flee plantations, showed his true sensibilities after the war when he took charge of the Great Abaco colony in the Bahamas, where freed Blacks had settled. American slave masters besieged Dunmore for the return of slaves who had evacuated with the British. Dunmore formed the "Negro Court" in 1787 and enticed Black people to appear and "claim their freedom." Out of thirty claimants, he returned twenty-nine to their former masters, their "lawful owners," as he called them, in violation of his own proclamation.[209]

Sir Guy Carleton, who had fought George Washington over the fate of escaped slaves loyal to King George, represented the opposite pole on the humanitarian scale. Carleton could have walked away when his side lost. The war was over, and there was nothing for him to gain professionally or militarily from advocating for the fair treatment of former slaves, and yet he did just that by winning concessions from George Washington. For keeping faith with the Black Loyalists, an enclave of 658 of them named their Bahamian settlement Carleton Point in recognition of the Englishman who honored his country's promise.[210]

In 1783, Corporal Washington disembarked from *L'Abondance*, one of many outbound British ships that sailed from the New York harbor, and set foot on Nova Scotian soil as a free man.[211] He was one of three thousand Black and white Loyalists who sought a new life in Canada, ready to avail themselves of royal land grants that would allow them to support themselves. Many of the white Loyalists had brought their slaves with them and were ready to reassert their American way of life under British rule. The government accommodated them with allotments of the most arable farmland.

The Black Loyalists were relegated to segregated areas of Nova Scotia, and land grants were slow in coming, smaller than promised, and located in rocky barren areas that could not support farming. Some received no land at all. They suffered through harsh winters, inadequate shelter, famine, and denial of voting and other civil rights. Most became share croppers or indentured servants for white landowners. Harry Washington was forced to hire himself out to white Loyalist landowners for low wages.[212]

After years of ill-treatment, the Black Loyalists petitioned the King for redress and were offered the opportunity to leave Nova Scotia and resettle in Sierra Leone. The British crown had granted a charter to the Sierra Leone Company for the establishment of a West African colony of free Blacks headed up by a governor and staff of white Englishmen. They named the colony Freetown. Relocating there would entitle the Black settlers to land grants for small farms. Roughly half of the original number of Black Nova Scotian settlers decided to emigrate to Sierra Leone, Harry Washington among them. By then, he was married to a woman named Jenny, and the couple had two small children.[213] At about age fifty, he was set to board another ship in search of freedom and security.

Men, women, and children prepared to leave Nova Scotia. Black Loyalist Boston King who, like Corporal Washington, had traveled to Nova Scotia aboard *L'Abondance,* prepared to resettle in Africa. A woman of 104 years of age begged to be taken onboard one of the ships "so that she might 'lay her bones in her native country.'" The company representative remarked that the former slaves who were ready to embark on a new life were not driven by "the idea of improving their own conditions, but for the sake of their children whom they wished to see established [. . .] upon a better foundation."[214]

In 1791, fifteen ships carrying 1,196 resettlers set sail for Africa. En route to Sierra Leone, the site of the British treaty negotiator Richard Oswald's slave fort, the African-born Harry Washington, must have felt he was going home, returning to the continent if not the country of his birth. The hopeful passengers disembarked, their feet touched the banks of the Sierra Leone River, and they sang: "The day of jubilee is come, return ye ransomed sinners home."[215] Corporal Washington, Jenny Washington, and their children carried their worldly possessions ashore—"an axe, saw and pickaxe, plus three hoes, as well as two muskets and several items of furniture"—ready to start a new life.[216]

Though the Sierra Leone Company named their settlement Freetown, to its owners, it was a profit-seeking enterprise like any other company. To the settlers, Freetown represented something more. Historian Sylvia Frey writes that the Black Loyalists "viewed themselves as heirs of the Revolution, [with expectations of] freedom from slavery for themselves and their families; the right to security in the small farms promised them and escape from the racial intolerance they discovered in [. . .] Nova Scotia [. . .] which constantly threatened their dignity and [. . .] freedom."[217]

While awaiting promised land allotments, the new settlers cleared jungle and constructed huts for shelter. Without land, they were at the mercy of the Sierra Leone Company, which extended them credit at the company store in lieu of wages for working on company land. After much protesting and petitioning, the settlers received land allotments, but only one-fifth the acreage that had been promised when they agreed to leave Nova Scotia.[218] The next dispute involved restricted water rights. The company denied the new settlers any land along the Sierra Leone River. The Black settlers had faced the same restriction in Nova Scotia—white owners of waterfront property charging Blacks for access to their private wharves for commerce. The company relented. The Black settlers gained access to the river and began farming their own land.

However, they soon learned that they were expected to pay quitrent (property tax) for the use of the land. The amount of quitrent demanded would have them paying an amount equal to the value of the land every twenty years. They argued so strenuously against paying the charge that for a time, the company did not extract it from them. The Black settlers then pressed company directors for the right to organize their society according to their values and needs by electing representatives and judges from among their numbers, a demand that echoed the unfairness denounced in the American revolutionary slogan "taxation without representation." They presented their argument in writing as best they could:

> They said they willingly agreed to be governed by the laws of England, but "we do not consent to gave it into your honer hands with out haven aney of our own culler in it" and reminded [Director] Clarkson he had promised them that "whoever came to Saraleon wold be free . . . and all should be equel," so it followed that they had "a wright to chuse men that we think proper for to act for us in a reasnenble manner."[219]

No doubt the Black Loyalists held these truths to be self-evident, but the company saw things differently. The directors found it odd that the resettled Black people considered themselves to be British subjects and charged them with "unwarranted pretensions [. . .] excessive jealousy of

Europeans [. . .] crude notions [. . .] of their own rights."[220] Just after the Black settlers presented their modest pleadings, the company became even more authoritarian and reasserted their demand for quitrent payments. Those who resisted were threatened with having their land allocations canceled. The company made note of troublemakers, and Harry Washington made the list. His fortunes once turned on finding his name written in *The Book of Negroes*; now he found himself included on a list of farmers in jeopardy of losing their livelihood.

A group of settlers held a meeting to discuss their situation, and so oppressive had the British governor of the colony become that he accused them of plotting against the company, charging them with sedition and treason. The governor adopted the role of plantation overseers and determined that the Black settlers' reasonable and very human quest for fair treatment was a criminal act. The company used its military to put down what they considered a rebellion.

Washington and a group of others were tried and convicted. Three men were executed. Washington and thirty-one other men were exiled from the colony and forced to live on their own in the undeveloped parts of Sierra Leone. He was about sixty years old at the time. He died within a few years.[221]

* * *

In Benjamin West's incomplete 1783 painting, Henry Laurens is barely there. Although his friend and slave-business associate Richard Oswald had arranged his bail, Laurens was held in the Tower of London as a prisoner of war until December of 1781, when he was exchanged for Lord Cornwallis, the British commander captured by the Americans at the Battle of Yorktown. Upon Laurens' release, General George Washington hailed him as "the father of our country."[222] Soon after his year of imprisonment, Laurens learned that his son had been killed in a minor battle in South Carolina. The news reached him in the same communiqué that contained his orders to go to Paris for treaty negotiations. His suffering and loss took a toll. His colleagues described him as sinking "into inertia" and looking "gaunt" upon his arrival in Paris.[223] And although his presence at the negotiating table was official, he was not one of the signatories to the treaty nor did he sit for the painting that includes him. The artist probably imagined Laurens' likeness based on previous portraits for which he had posed. Blaming ill health, Laurens left Paris immediately after making his contribution to the treaty.

The American signatories later commented on Laurens' revision of Article 7. John Adams, who looks somewhat insubstantial in the painting, opposed slavery and was the only one of the American signatories who never owned slaves. Yet he held a cavalier attitude toward the implications of Laurens' amendment. Adams wrote in his diary: "Mr. Laurens said there ought to be a Stipulation that the British Troops should carry off no Negroes or other American Property. We all agreed. Mr. Oswald consented. Then The Treaties were signed, sealed and delivered, and We all went out to Passy to dine with Dr. Franklin. Thus far has proceeded this great Affair."[224]

John Jay owned slaves by inheritance but was a committed abolitionist who had tried to have slavery outlawed in his home state of New York. Subsequent to signing the treaty, Jay denounced the Article 7 addition as "immoral."[225] He went on to become governor of his state, and in that capacity, he signed the 1799 Act for the Gradual Abolition of Slavery into law.[226] Jay is regally posed in West's painting, standing on the far-left side, holding a scroll in his right hand. An oddity, his left hand is raised waist-high and pointed toward the interior space of the painting, his index finger appearing to almost touch the seated Benjamin Franklin's shoulder but perhaps directed at the standing Henry Laurens, the father of Article 7.

Benjamin Franklin, without commenting specifically on Article 7, told a friend that "the events of the day [of the signing of the treaty] had made him happier than he had ever hoped to be at his age." For forty years, Franklin owned slaves. He did not become an abolitionist until near the end of his life.[227]

John Jay's biographer surmises that Jay, Franklin, and Adams conceded to Laurens' demand in order to "secure [S]outhern support for the treaty," Laurens being the lone Southerner among them.[228]

Just before the treaty was signed, British negotiator Richard Oswald was replaced. On signing day, David Hartley represented Great Britain. No changes were made to the treaty before the signing, but it is noteworthy that, unlike his slave-owning predecessor, Hartley opposed slavery and, as a member of the British Parliament, had put forward legislation for its abolition.[229] Benjamin West planned to include the British signer in his 1783 painting. The big messy blotch on the right side of the canvas was to have been filled with David Hartley's likeness, but he declined, sending word to the artist that he considered himself "too ugly" to pose. West abandoned his painting in its incomplete state.

In September of 2008, at Baltimore's historic Carroll Mansion, the Maryland chapter of the Sons of the American Revolution unveiled a David R. Wagner oil painting, a reimagining of Benjamin West's then 225-year-old painting commemorating the signing of the Treaty of Paris.[230] Over two centuries later, the contemporary artist takes some liberties with his own painting, filling in some blanks in order to flesh out a new, more complete version. On the right side of the new canvas, the domed United States Capitol Building rises in the background under a colorful sky. The dark mass that looked like ominous wings hovering above the men in the eighteenth-century painting is maroon drapery in the new one. John Jay's right hand still clutches a scroll, but he no longer points a finger at anyone with his left hand, which is now hidden behind John Adams's back. The seated Adams looks more substantial, yet somehow thinner. The seated Benjamin Franklin, holding an upright quill in his left hand, is dressed in a proper frock coat like the other American gentlemen, but still bareheaded without a powdered wig. Henry Laurens, the sometimes tardy, sometimes absent non-signer, stands at the center of the canvas as if presiding. And the Englishman, David Hartley, is conjured from the beyond with oil paints to haunt the previous void. He sits at the right side of the treaty table, wearing an embellished red cloak with white collar. His piercing, quizzical eyes seem to ask, *How the devil did I get here?* Or, abolitionist that he was, he could be questioning Article 7.

* * *

In 1793, George Washington signed the country's first fugitive slave law, allowing runaway slaves captured in any state to be forced back into slavery.[231] But many of his contemporaries, with much lesser political standing than president of the United States, called for abolition. Several Northern states passed laws mandating gradual emancipation. Pennsylvania passed its Gradual Abolition Act a decade before

George and Martha Washington moved to the United States capital in Philadelphia, where they lived for seven years. The law called for the automatic manumission of slaves after they resided in the state for six months. This created a dilemma for the president and first lady, as they had brought nine of their slaves from their Mount Vernon plantation in Virginia to serve them in the executive mansion.

Rather than comply with the spirit of the law, the couple conspired. As the president's slaves neared the six-month mark, George sent them back to Mount Vernon for a temporary stay, or Martha would take them across the state line for a brief period. The six-month clock would then restart upon the slaves' return to Philadelphia. When George hatched his plan, he asked for secrecy, writing to his personal secretary, "I request that these Sentiments and this advise [sic] may be known to none but yourself & Mrs. Washington."[232]

Despite the fugitive slave law, Harry Washington remained out of George Washington's legal reach. During a brief period when Corporal Washington would have been in his fifties, before the Sierra Leone governor criminalized the aspirations of the settlers, his future looked promising. He became a successful farmer, raising coffee, pepper, and ginger for trade. He was able to support himself and his family by trading and raising his own staples like rice and yams.

While still in Nova Scotia, Boston King converted to Methodism and became a preacher. He went on to build a congregation in his new home of Sierra Leone and opened a school where he taught the children of the settlers. The Washingtons' children were no doubt among them. King's efforts were encouraged and rewarded when the company sent him to a Methodist school in England to further his education. After two years, he returned to Sierra Leone and resumed his preaching and teaching career.[233]

Once Corporal Washington established his own farm, he named it Mount Vernon. A professor of history mentions this in a recent article, writing that he adopted that name "in honor of his former master."[234] I think the professor's assumption is as false as George Washington's powdered wig.

No one can know what led him to choose this name for his land: a sly cynicism, to which he would have been righteously entitled, or a grand sense of justice, or a symbolic way of achieving a tiny bit of balance, or a sense of humor the size of the continent of his birth, or the desire to daily celebrate himself as a family man and owner of his land and his person? Having learned about this man's journey, I would guess that there was some measure of all of these yearnings and more embodied in Harry Washington's Mount Vernon, and that he chose the name to honor himself.

PART FOUR

The Heart is a Muscle

When my future husband Ted was fifteen, he was scrawny and cute. I didn't know him then, but he tells me he didn't care much for those labels. He couldn't do anything about his age, but there was a cure for scrawny and cute.

Many of the comic books he read—*Captain America, The Green Hornet, Batman*—featured ads with pictures of Charles Atlas and other muscle men flexing and bulging and promising that "you too can be a husky he-man." Southern California, where Ted lived at the time, was the center of the bodybuilding universe, and for a modest fee, the insecure adolescent could mail-order a kind of owner's manual for the male body. It was the early 1960s when Ted ordered his first bodybuilding books and set out to build himself a body.

He bought a set of used weights with earnings from his weekend job at a catering shop, hammered some old wood together for a weight bench, and got started on his new body. Primal grunts and clanging metal noises emanated from the garage at all hours as Ted tortured himself with ever increasing poundage. His weight set totaled one hundred pounds, and his initial goal was to lift all of those pounds overhead at one time. He made incremental progress, but his goal eluded him. He reached a point at which he could lift seventy-five, then eighty-five pounds, and then he hit ninety—but he would crumble under the final ten.

After some weeks, he set out to trick himself. He placed all of the weights on one bar before leaving for school. The set up weighed one hundred pounds, but all day long he told himself that ninety pounds awaited him at home. All day, the future psychology minor said to himself, "Only ninety pounds . . . I know I can do ninety pounds." He came in from school, went directly to the garage, and hoisted the one hundred pounds of iron with no problem. Then he repped it a few times just to show off in front of himself. There was no stopping him now.

He pumped and lifted and bench-pressed and wheezed, and as more weeks went by, he could stand before a mirror, something he did often, flex a bicep, and see something that was definitely bigger than a zit. Yes, definitely, this was progress.

He persevered. Friends took notice. Seeing the transformation, some of them decided they too wanted to look he-mannish like Ted. They contributed more weights to Ted's garage gym, and soon the place was filled with enough equipment for a new iron age on Riverside, California's Park Avenue. Ted's garage became a magnet for the Black and Chicano boys of the neighborhood. They gathered there to work on their ongoing metamorphoses into manhood. Here, all vestiges of scrawny and cute could be mashed out of them by the sheer weight of iron. They continually challenged themselves. In joyous pain, they piled on more and more weight and endured ever-increasing reps.

Ted expanded his gym to accommodate the budding cadre of body builders, though he was careful to leave his little brother's train set undisturbed on its table-top tracks. He commandeered more raw materials, built a few more benches, and fixed more rope pulleys to the walls. They worked out with the big garage door open, the aroma of orange groves and pesticides mingling with fumes of sweat and testosterone and the grunting noises of determined boys. They worked the pulleys and pullers, hundreds of pounds of iron, dumbbells and barbells, with Beethoven blasting in the background. Beethoven? Yes, Bradley, one of the other Black kids, insisted on classical music for his workouts.

Ted's mom told him she approved of his pursuit. She was neutral about the physical side of it, but she appreciated the cultural infusion. Her son was getting exposed to classical music, and he was learning Spanish from Navarro and the other Chicano boys. Little did Mom know that Bradley was a part-time thug with a thin Beethoven veneer, and Ted's new Spanish vocabulary consisted of curse words and a few colorful ways of expressing "what's up" or "right on, dude" or "you're a pitiful idiot." *Que paso, simon ese, pinche pendejo.*

They isolated and nicknamed pairs of muscles—lats, delts, traps, pecs, glutes, wings—and targeted them for torture with curls, squats, bench presses, standing presses, and Ted's makeshift lat machine: a contraption that required a pulling-down motion to strengthen the latissimus dorsi. They celebrated each other's great moments in weightlifting, and as their muscle mass increased, so did their confidence and facial hair. The garage had no mirrors, but they could step outside to pose and put on a flex fest in front of the big reflective windows on the side of the house a few yards away.

* * *

By age sixteen, Ted was a gloriously out-of-proportion human being like the specimens on the backs of his comic books—a muscular triangle on legs. Charles Atlas had inspired him to become, as he put it, "Charles At Last!" He and his friends kept to their workout schedule, and everyone progressed.

One afternoon, when there were about ten Black and brown iron-pumping young men in the gym garage, a challenge spontaneously arose. They would do standing presses with one hundred pounds, "cleaning and pressing" the weight from the floor to shoulder height, then press the bar overhead. From that position, they would do as many overhead reps as they could. Each one took a turn heaving the barbell and repping, each trying to top the strength and endurance of the others. One by one, they began to drop out of the little contest as they reached their physical limits—"maxed out," they called it—and soon it was down to two of them: Ted and Navarro.

Ted racked up eight reps with one hundred pounds and looked as though he might still have more fight in him. Then it was Navarro's turn to challenge that. He attacked the barbell with great determination, jerked and pumped and pressed, and topped Ted with nine reps.

"On you, Ted."

The others, the maxed-out onlookers, cheered Ted on. He made the most awful faces and frightful noises as he took on the evil iron, braced himself under it, and thrust the iron aloft. He met Navarro's challenge and topped it with ten reps. His shoulders and arms burned so, he imagined them going up in flames. Now all eyes were on the challenger.

"On you, Navarro."

Navarro gnashed his teeth and approached the weight. The onlookers went into a frenzy. Navarro was going for eleven reps. He sucked in all of the available oxygen in the place, positioned himself, snatched then swung the bar to his chest, and pressed it overhead. Right around his fourth or fifth rep, in between the general bursts of auditory macho, one voice in the group suddenly stood out. It was not very loud, but filled with passion.

"*La Raza*," the voice said.

Others joined in: "*La Raza*." Each time Navarro pressed the iron over his head, the chanting coming from the Chicano boys crescendoed. "*La Raza . . . ! La Raza . . . ! La Raza!*"

Navarro hit his eleventh rep in triumph. He had met Ted's challenge and topped it by one, and he received the affirmation befitting a victorious warrior from his Chicano brethren.

There were roughly equal numbers of Black and brown boys present. Ted looked on as Navarro slapped hands with the Chicano boys, some of whom were still chanting "*La Raza!*" Ted thought about this new element that had just injected itself into their competition. The gym garage had never before been a place where one's race was at issue. Suddenly, the Black boys were all looking to Ted. He took in the whole scene—the triumphant Chicano boys and the anxious-looking, maxed-out Black onlookers suddenly in need of racial validation. He drew in his third wind and approached the barbell. He was going for the twelve reps. A voice, this time it was a Black voice in the crowd, joyously decreed, "The Splibs are still in it!" The Black boys, not having a chant that was the equivalent of "*La Raza*," urged Ted on by shouting out the number of each rep.

"One. . . . Two. . . ."

Ted grimaced and lifted, seeming to gain strength from the excitement of the others.

"Three. . . . Four. . . ."

He wasn't tired. He felt certain he could do twelve reps if he held his concentration. But other thoughts crowded his head. As he rhythmically pressed the barbell again and again to the beat of the count, he was aware of his discomfort in this new role of race savior. He had taken up bodybuilding for his own gratification, to feel good about himself and maybe attract some girls. It was never about winners and losers. Now, he was being called on to save the honor of his people, a burden Black children of the time seemed to absorb through their very skin.

"Five. . . . Six. . . ."

His mind raced. What would it be like if he won? A show of righteous arrogance from his Black friends, depression and dejection for his Chicano friends.

"Seven. . . . Eight. . . ."

If he lost, he would have failed his people. It would be on his head.

"Nine. . . . Ten. . . ."

One more rep to tie Navarro, two more to top him. Ted considered stopping at eleven reps.

The twelfth rep might divide what was one group into two. Maybe forever.

But what if he stopped there and Navarro came back and did twelve reps, and Ted, having to start all over again, proved unable to match that? Then he and all of the Black boys would be losers. On the other hand, Navarro's biceps and shoulders must have been flaming from those eleven reps. Would he be able to start at number one again and get to twelve?

"Eleven. . . ."

Ted dropped his hundred-pound burden to the floor.

He was certain that he still had another rep in him, yet he chose not to go for it. He pinned his eyes on Navarro, wondering if he had anything left to give for *La Raza*. Navarro met his gaze and smiled, and then, instead of going for the barbell, he went in for a hug. A manly one. He and Ted, along with the others, celebrated a victorious tie.

Everyday Ekphrasis

Culinary Art

Emily's chocolate cake exudes its gentle brown magic consuming the consumer. Emily's chocolate cake is the anti-vanilla, a velvety black hole blanketing out sound, subsuming and negating its crystal white ingredients noiselessly, hungrily, and sending fruit flavors into a parallel universe where rainbow-colored flavors live riotously in unending daylight away from the thick bittersweet chocolate hush. Emily's chocolate cake is a comforting eclipse, reassurance that darkness will follow light.

The Cardboard Box

Sometimes, when you are overcome by the silliness of uncontrollable laughter, you set off a contagion and others in your company will laugh too, even without knowing what it is that you find so funny. Not this time. People stared blank-faced. Ted shot me a confused and worried look, a look that said that he might be considering something like involuntary commitment for his hysterical wife.

We were touring an exhibition called *Lifelike* at the New Orleans Museum of Art.

Appropriate. It was my first outing after three weeks as a shut-in waylaid by flu, and I was at last feeling lifelike myself. The exhibit consisted of everyday objects rendered as art—Andy Warhol's giant *Brillo Box* sculptures, Jonathan Seliger's *Heartland,* a nine-foot-tall milk carton. But there were some really odd ones too: a large white trash bag slouching on the floor, full and lumpy and cinched up at the top; a blue sleeping bag sprawled on the floor and contoured to suggest a body inside; a bundle of stacked newspapers tied with string; a large square of cardboard leaning on the wall, which was entitled *still. life. (cardboard leaning on the wall).*

People milled around the exhibit rooms appreciating art all over the place, but I couldn't quite work up any enthusiasm for those mundane objects. I was feeling put upon, coerced into seeing art where there was no art, just stuff. Then I turned away from one of these objects and found myself looking at a small cardboard box mounted at eye level on the sterile white wall—a ratty little box that looked as if the UPS man had manhandled it badly—water-stained and held together by crudely torn strips of masking tape. Faced with something that belonged in the recycling bin, I burst into uncontrollable laughter. That's when Ted gave me that look of genuine concern.

I covered my mouth with my hand, but the laughter escaped. I had to get away from that box pronto, so I moved quickly into the next room, laughing and coughing and wheezing and trying to gulp down some air. Finally I calmed down, and Ted came after me, looking to find out what had set me off. I opened my mouth to say something to him, and out poured more giggles. I was in trouble, unable to even speak the words "cardboard" and "box" to Ted. I walked away.

Once I had calmed myself again, I looked at more lifelike art in another room. I was doing okay until I came upon some pieces of paint-flecked lumber and rags strewn haphazardly on the floor in the corner. *Some workmen must have left this here,* I thought. Tacky. But no, oh no. There was a plaque on the floor next to this jumble and a "Do Not Touch" sign. *Oh my God, it's art!* The giggles began to build again, and I had to get out of there, away from the art and the serious people. When Ted caught up with me again, I was finally able to speak.

"When I saw that cardboard box mounted on the wall, I could feel the artist mocking me," I said.

I told him that my mind flashed to a sort of convention I'd seen in movies, a shorthand used to portray a character as a pretentious fool. Just place that person in an art gallery and have them comment on an object thought to be art displayed on a wall, only to learn that they've been staring at a thermostat or a heating vent as they opined away like an art critic. When my eyes met the box, I went into a state of super-self-consciousness. I suddenly felt like I'd been set up to look like that fool, and it was just too funny. Hearing my breathless explanation, Ted shook his head from side to side and looked puzzled. He failed to see the humor but seemed less inclined to have me put away.

I knew I would have to write about the experience and wanted to know the name of the artist who elevated the cardboard box into the realm of art. I couldn't risk getting close enough to the box to get the information, afraid I'd erupt in laughter again, so I asked Ted to fetch it.

Later, I dispassionately researched the *Lifelike* exhibit and learned that things were not at all as they seemed. Not at all. Ugo Rondinone's *still. life. (cardboard leaning on the wall)* is not cardboard at all; it is made of bronze and lead painted to look exactly like a big piece of cardboard refuse.[235] The lumpy trash bag entitled *Hefty 2-Ply* is actually a Renaissance-style marble carving by Jud Nelson, and while it looks light enough to sling over your shoulder, it actually weighs 1,500 pounds.[236] Hefty, indeed. The plush-looking blue sleeping bag with a body imprint is a painted bronze casting by Gavin Turk entitled *Nomad*.[237] The bundled newspapers tied with twine are used as a medium to which artist Robert Gober adds graphics that, together with headlines and text, tell a story on the topmost layer of newsprint; the technique is called photolithography.[238]

That strewn pile of wood that drove me from the exhibit is one of many such three-dimensional installation art pieces by Susan Collis; *Forever Young*, the one I took for construction junk, is composed of planks of ebony, studded with white gold and inlays of mother-of-pearl and other gem fragments to suggest nail heads and paint spatter; the stains on the drop cloth are made of thread—blobs hand-embroidered by the artist.[239] And the cardboard box that was my undoing is a work by Daniel Douke entitled *Bucklin*; it is constructed of sturdy Masonite and painted with acrylics.[240] Much work went into the creation of that beat-up little package. The color of the cardboard, the water stains, the "this end up" arrows, the jagged-edged masking tape—all of these details done in paint render the object so faithfully as to inspire a kind of hysteria in certain people.

A local reviewer wrote about the exhibit, "The art in *Lifelike* not only fools the eye, it ties the eye's shoelaces together and steals its lunch money."[241] Having learned the truth about what I was looking at, I have to agree with that assessment. I re-evaluate the cardboard box now as I look at it on my computer screen. What makes a work of art successful? Is the piece creative and well executed? Check. Memorable? Check. Does it foster a connection between artist and viewer? Check. Does it entertain? Hahahahaha. . . . *check*.

The Ring

A winged metal tube slices through clouds thirty-five thousand feet up. Sealed inside, sharing the same recycled air, strangers make up a temporary community, united around the common wish for a safe landing and maybe some extra peanuts. We pass the time interacting with travel mates, reading, hooked up to earphones, getting lost in observing scenes inside and outside the airplane. In the scuffle of boarding, I notice a portly man moving up the aisle. I see the flash of something huge and gold and gem-encrusted on his hand, worn like a ring but spreading across many fingers. I try to get a better look, but he moves out of range. The monstrosity on his finger has enough gold and diamonds to be a bracelet. A very small person could maybe wear it like a tiara.

The bejeweled man settles into his aisle seat. I've managed to score an aisle seat myself on the opposite side about five rows back. I study the thing on his left hand as he rests it on the arm of his seat. He's a little too far away for me to make out details of the hunk of metal and stones attached to him like a growth, but I can see that the diamonds form an asymmetrical pattern and appear to spell out something in letters.

We've brought our earthly attitudes along. The sheer size of the ring, the number of diamonds it clutches, invites judgment, and I pull mine out like I'm unsheathing a knife. If this is his idea of a monogram, then his ego must be the size of this plane. I condemn this ostentatious display while, at the same time, I wonder why this man is flying coach. He could afford his own plane, or at least a couple of first-class seats—one for himself and one for his jewelry. What does he do? How is he taking in so much money that he can flaunt his wealth with this brass knuckle of a ring? I decide that he has to be either a crook or a capitalist pig. Same difference, really.

I bide my time. I wonder, I judge, but finally I'm so maddeningly curious to see what the diamonds spell out that I plot my course to the forward bathroom. I move slowly, keeping my eyes pinned to the ring, hoping he doesn't decide to make any sudden gestures that would blur my view. And there it is. I'm close enough to see it, to read the diamonds. "F-U-C-K—Y-O-U," the message reads. I wince. *Fuck you* in diamonds, thrown in my face by this haughty bastard who has anticipated my judgment and had his response ready and waiting, his opinion of the opinionator close at hand, so to speak. He's caught me.

He's won. And all he had to do was sit there with his hand attached to his arm. Something like mild shock registers. And then I find the whole thing funny. Really funny.

Passengers observing a woman on her way to the bathroom no doubt wonder why she's grinning and stifling giggles. They are free to make up explanations for this odd behavior, free to judge her and then let their earthly thoughts wander elsewhere in the clouds.

Can an Umbrella Be Said to Have a Patina?

Aunt Phil saved old fabric scraps to make quilts in her spare time, beautiful and utilitarian creations. She treated other possessions like quilt pieces as well, objects to be saved for some future purpose. She worked at her job into her seventies, even as arthritis challenged her every step, and she came to rely on a sturdy, black-lacquered walking stick with a pistol grip.

I regularly took her to doctors' appointments and to make groceries, and if rain was forecast, she carried a large umbrella along with her walking stick. The cloth of the umbrella had the patina of age, an off-black, soft matte finish. The well-worn curved handle was made of bone-colored plastic with tan streaks etched in to mimic carved wood. The umbrella was the same length as her walking stick, and the two objects handled together in one hand, purse in the other hand, made for awkward ambulation. For her birthday one year, I gave her a folding umbrella, the kind that collapses down to a fraction of its unfurled self, small enough to fit inside a purse. The birthday umbrella was red—her favorite color—and her face glowed when she unwrapped it.

"Red!" she exclaimed, just as she always did when she unwrapped any red gift.

But I never saw her use the new umbrella. I'd pick her up on a day when the weatherman had predicted rain, and she'd descend the steps of her front porch with the walking cane and her old black umbrella, just as if I'd never given her my brilliant gift. I didn't question her about it. She was my elder, my aunt, my godmother—someone to whom I would perpetually be a child. It would have been impertinent to ask her for a rationale.

Aunt Phil was widowed and had no children of her own, and so when she died at the age of ninety, it fell to her nieces to sort through her things. I was with my cousin Rhonda the day we found the red folding umbrella, still in its original plastic in Aunt Phil's bottom dresser drawer. Next to it were two more folding umbrellas, a blue one and a plaid one. Rhonda recognized one of them as a gift she had given Aunt Phil years before. All three had the shiny patina of newness, of never-been-usedness. We stared at the umbrellas for a moment, puzzling over the habits of our frugal, beloved elder, a cautious woman who was saving her new umbrellas for a rainy day.

Inventory
One two-tiered end table: Hand-crafted by Joe Dyer, who died when his son was eight and his daughter was six. Lightweight, possibly pine; recently re-shellacked; drawer stuck due to poor re-shellacking job; table is now holding up a plant on top and, on the bottom, a chess set, a red cloth box containing Chinese Baoding balls, a New Orleans tour guide book, and a cookie can containing their late mother's rock collection; dust on top and bottom.

One rectangular, two-tiered occasional table: Hand-crafted by Joe Dyer, who died when his son was eight and his daughter was six. Possibly oak; now holding up a jumble of bedroom things on top and their late mother's Bible and some books to sell on Amazon on the bottom; dust on top, bottom, and Bible.

One small, two-shelf bookcase: Hand-crafted by Joe Dyer, who died when his son was eight and his daughter was six. Wood of unknown origin; now holding Joe's daughter's cookbooks, all dusty except *The Joy of Cooking.*

One large cedar chest: Hand-crafted by Joe Dyer, who died when his son was eight and his daughter was six. Solid cedar, very heavy; removable lid also heavy; chest imparts cedar fragrance to anything placed in it; velvety raw wood inside; deep reddish-brown varnish outside resembling Joe in color; a series of hard right angles and threatening corners, unlike Joe; wide wooden base causes cedar chest to protrude into pathway; base of chest has a history of shearing off toes, hence chest's banishment to the attic; Joe's children grew up with it above their heads; chest now lives at

Joe's daughter's home, where it holds memories of fragrant new wood, wispy sawdust, and curled pine shavings, Joe's laughter heard over shrill power-tool whine, and a father's love of wood and children, usually not in that order.

Black Eye of the Beholder

We round the corner of Pirate's Alley and walk among the sidewalk artists in the plaza in front of St. Louis Cathedral in the French Quarter. I happen upon a painting that I can't look away from. Propped on an easel and looking back at me is an oil painting of a little Black boy of about five or six years old. His baby face is questioning and trusting at the same time. His left arm is reaching upwards, and his little hand is caught and held by a strong, fatherly hand that extends down from the sleeve of a denim jacket. The top of the painting ends just above the cuff of the man's sleeve. The strong brown hand, the hard-working denim—that's all we'll ever see of the man.

It doesn't matter who might stroll into the boy's field of vision; his message will be the right one for whomever his trusting brown eyes enchant. He tells me about my childhood. My own father died when I was about the boy's age. My father was out of the picture as the man is out of the painting, but, like the denim-sleeved dad, still there, distant and close.

I soak it all in slowly. The artist is a genius. I want to adopt this child. Next, I have to descend from this high place where art has lifted me and do the prosaic thing. I have to look at the price tag. I can't believe it—a two-digit price dangles from the frame. Must buy, must own, will cherish. Ted says yes, we can do this and still make the rent. Ted is a genius. I will take this sweet little boy home with me, and we can look at each other every day.

I locate the artist, a middle-aged white woman, and I tell her that I'm ready to buy her creation. Her lips tighten, her eyes narrow, her brow wrinkles. I repeat my offer. She says, "You want to buy this painting?", and it sounds like a dare. Then she gives me a price that's high up in the three digits. There's some mistake. I point to the two-digit price on the frame.

She says, "That's the price of the frame, not the painting," and in my head I hear her add, *you idiot.*

I cannot respond with anything but an embarrassed, "Oh."

I bid the boy a sad farewell, and turning to leave, I come face to face with the president of the United States—the Republican one from the 1980s—fleshed out on canvas. The oily likeness of Ronald Reagan is a creation of the same artist, done with the same level of skill as the painting of the boy. The president is angled toward me on an easel, grinning, laughing maybe.

My spirit turns mean and scornful for artist and subject. Here was the president who tried to have ketchup declared a vegetable so that funding for the school lunch program could be cut, who tried to classify burial plots as real estate so that elderly people could be kicked off food stamps for exceeding the financial resource limit, whose spending deficit equaled that of all previous presidents combined, whose trickle-down economics meant a trickling-up of wealth.

The two paintings clash in my mind. The artist who honored this president must have created the bewitching boy by accident, and she probably doesn't even know what that painting means, and she must be an art thief, and she couldn't possibly understand what the boy and the man and the denim sleeve would symbolize to a person with tender feelings like mine. And what kind of fine artist spends her time painting Republicans, anyway? Not even for a one-digit price would I have anything of hers in my rented home, delivering her judgment through the lifelike eyes of a painting.

It wasn't just that she insulted us with that sneer and that tone; it wasn't just that she cast Ted and me on sight as creatures so ignorant of art that we expected to purchase an original oil painting for the price of a frame; it wasn't just that she was right in that assessment of us—although that was very hard to take. There was more. This woman shattered the mystique of the artist that I had held unconsciously up until that day. From then on, I would have to separate art from artist.

Ode on a Grecian Sentence

> Those blanks to be filled are like the variables in an algebraic equation, a network of complex relationships, their meaning determined largely by superposition, juxtaposition, and a literary order of operations that requires the computation of

> successive disparate parts individually first, and then in small groups, and finally as one large whole—a lyric equation of the quadratic order, the results of which depended upon the data provided by the reader, but which all reside on the same curve of meaning, subjective iteration of the primary form envisioned by the author.[242]

This sentence-on-steroids was chiseled by Joey Franklin for his article "Essaying the Thing: An Imagiste Approach to the Lyric Essay," wherein he boldly promotes the mathification of creative nonfiction. The sentence is neither left- nor right-brained, but some ambidextrous-brained, Frankenstein-esque entity.

Help! Make it stop.

This hybrid creature, this ginormous algebraic construct dressed in words, lurks inside the pages of the September 2012 *Writer's Chronicle,* from whence it stalks unsuspecting English majors. Frightening. We need to take out a restraining order against this sentence.

Please keep your math out of my English, Joey Franklin. This is not a happy accidental pairing, like getting your peanut butter in my chocolate. This is bilinear intimidation, a terrifying pronouncement that halts the free-flow of language, restricting its movement, freezing it like the human figures on Keats's urn. This sentence might as well be Greek.

Run, English majors! Save yourselves!

Endnotes

The Resistance

1. D. C. O'Dowd, memorandum, 1928, Order no. 1128, New Orleans Streetcar Conductors, Adjusting Race Screens, New Orleans, reissued 1945, archived February 24, 2001 at https://web.archive.org/web/20010224035449/http://nutrias.org/~nopl/exhibits/ccmem/5.htm, web; *Crescent City Memories Exhibit* at the New Orleans Public Library, April 10, 2015.
2. "Trio Ignited Controlled Revolution in the '70's," *The Louisiana Weekly*, archived November 24, 2004, at https://web.archive.org/web/20041124052258/http://www.louisianaweekly.com/cgi-bin/weekly/news/articlegate.pl?20030526j#expand.
3. "Desire Lines," Academic Dictionaries and Encyclopedia, archived May 26, 2022, at https://web.archive.org/web/20240917091547/https://en-academic.com/dic.nsf/enwiki/2700170.
4. "Desire Lines," Academic Dictionaries and Encyclopedias.
5. Lisa Rein, "Mystery of Va.'s First Slaves is Unlocked 400 Years Later," *The Washington Post*, September 3, 2006, http://www.washingtonpost.com/wpdyn/content/article/2006/09/02/AR2006090201097.html (site discontinued); William Edward Hartpole Lecky, *A History of England in the Eighteenth Century* (Nabu Press, 2010), vol. 4, quoted in "Origins of the Slave Trade," The Web of English History, archived December 2, 2024, at https://web.archive.org/web/20241202145159/https://www.historyhome.co.uk/readings/slavery.htm; "Sir John Hawkins," NNBD, archived December 10, 2024, at https://web.archive.org/web/20241210054555/https://nndb.com/people/186/000101880/#expand.

6. Howard Zinn, *A People's History of the United States* (HarperCollins, 2010), 26, Google Play Books; Lyon Gardiner, ed., *Tyler's Quarterly and Genealogical Magazine*, vol. 1 (Whittet and Shepperson Printers, 1920), Google Play Books; Richard S. Dunn, James Savage, and Laetitia Yeandle, eds., "The Journal of John Winthrop 1630–1649" (University Press, 1996), 246, quoted in "African Americans and the End of Slavery in Massachusetts," Massachusetts Historical Society, https://www.masshist.org/endofslavery/index.php.
7. Gilles Deleuze, "On Capitalism and Desire," quoted in Matthew Tiessen, "Accepting Invitations: Desire Lines as Earthly Offerings," *Rhizomes*, 15 (2007): https://web.archive.org/web/20240802130319/http://rhizomes.net/issue15/tiessen.html.
8. Cynthia Jacobs Carter, ed., *Freedom in My Heart: Voices From the United States National Slavery Museum* (National Geographic Books, 2008), 78.
9. "Slave Ships," World is Afrika, archived May 10, 2004, at https://web.archive.org/web/20040510211244/http://home.btclick.com/jabu/ships.htm; Lucille Clifton, "slaveships," Poetry Foundation, accessed April 11, 2014, https://www.poetryfoundation.org/poems/55275/slaveships; Lisa Rein, "Mystery of Va.'s First Slaves is Unlocked 400 Years Later," *The Washington Post*, September 3, 2006, http://www.washingtonpost.com/wpdyn/content/article/2006/09/02/AR2006090201097.html (site discontinued); Christopher Minster, "10 Facts About Pirate 'Black Bart' Roberts," ThoughtCo., archived January 30, 2025, at https://web.archive.org/web/20250130095600/https://www.thoughtco.com/facts-about-pirate-black-bart-roberts-2136237.
10. Lisa Maloney, "Glossary of Hiking Terms," archived November 12, 2024, at https://web.archive.org/web/20241112100321/https://hikingalaska.net/2021/02/10/glossary-of-hiking-terms-and-backpacking-lingo/.
11. John F. Collin, *Political Affairs of the Country* (M. Parker Williams, Register and Gazette Office, 1883), 3: 4–5; Wendy Anne Warren, "The Cause of Her Grief: The Rape of a Slave in Early New England," *The Journal of American History*, 93, no. 4 (2007): 1031–49, https://doi.org/10.2307/25094595.
12. Warren, "The Cause of Her Grief," 1039.

13. "Slavery in Massachusetts," Slavery in the North, archived February 20, 2004, at https://web.archive.org/web/20040220231542/http://slavenorth.com/massachusetts.htm#expand; "First Baptist Church in America," Pluralism Project Archive, updated October 11, 2009, https://hwpi.harvard.edu/pluralismarchive/first-baptist-church-america.
14. "Pequot War," CTHumanities, archived December 04, 2024, at https://web.archive.org/web/20241204235929/https://connecticuthistory.org/topics-page/pequot-war/.
15. "Desire Lines," Academic Dictionaries and Encyclopedia.
16. "Desiree," Think Baby Names, accessed April 11, 2014, https://web.archive.org/web/20240920024529/https://www.thinkbabynames.com/meaning/0/Desiree.
17. Ned Hémard, "Remembering New Orleans History, Culture and Traditions: Hidden Desires," New Orleans Bar Association: New Orleans Nostalgia, accessed April 11, 2014, http://99ebook.com/read-file/hidden-desire-1-21-new-orleans-bar-association-pdf-2091593/ (site discontinued); "Desiree's Birth Year," Ancestry, accessed January 12, 2014, http://wiz.ancestry.com/wiz/Results#record>.
18. John La Plante, "Desire Lines Indicate Yearning," quoted in Patricia Leigh Brown, "Ideas & Trends; Whose Sidewalk Is It, Anyway?," *The New York Times*, January 5, 2003, https://www.nytimes.com/2003/01/05/weekinreview/ideas-trends-whose-sidewalk-is-it-anyway.html.
19. Matthew Tiessen, "Urban Meanderhals and the City of 'Desire Lines,'" CTHEORY, https://web.archive.org/web/20160314010444/https://journals.uvic.ca/index.php/ctheory/article/view/14515/5358.
20. Guillory Family History, Ancestry, accessed April 14, 2014, https://www.ancestry.com/name-origin?surname=guillory.
21. Patti Digh, *Life is a Verb: 37 Days to Wake Up, Be Mindful, and Live Intentionally* (Globe Pequot, 2008), 172.

The Problem We All Live With

22. Katy Reckdahl, "Fifty Years Later, Students Recall Integrating New Orleans Public School," *The Times-Picayune*, November 13, 2010, https://www.nola.com/news/politics/fifty-years-later-students-

recall-integrating-new-orleans-public-schools/article_c087accd-5bb7-5940-b062-8deadb53d0fc.html.

23. "Remembering Ruby Bridges," Publishing the Long Civil Rights Movement, accessed October 14, 2015, https://web.archive.org/web/20150921173323/https://lcrm.lib.unc.edu/blog/index.php/tag/william-frantz-elementary-school/.

24. John Steinbeck, *Travels with Charley in Search of America* (Viking Press, 1962), 194–95.

25. John Updike, "Comment," *The New Yorker*, December 2, 1960, https://www.newyorker.com/magazine/1960/12/10/comment-4710.

26. "Norman Rockwell Biography and Artwork," The Artchive, updated April 11, 2023, https://www.artchive.com/artists/norman-rockwell/.

27. J. D. De Blieux, et al., *The New Orleans School Crisis: Reports of the Louisiana State Advisory Committee to the United States Commissions on Civil Rights* (The University of Maryland School of Law, 1961), https://web.archive.org/web/20120824071602/http://www.crm-vet.org/docs/ccr_new_orleans_schools.pdf.

28. Plater Robinson, *A House Divided: A Teaching Guide on the History of Civil Rights in Louisiana*, 2nd ed. (The Southern Institute for Education and Research, 1995), http://www.southerninstitute.info/civil_rights_education/divided10.html.

29. De Bilieux, *The New Orleans School Crisis*.

30. Richard Severo, "Jimmie Davis, Louisiana's Singing Governor, Is Dead," *The New York Times*, November 6, 2000, https://www.nytimes.com/2000/11/06/us/jimmie-davis-louisiana-s-singing-governor-is-dead.html?pagewanted=all&src=pm.

31. Reckdahl, "Fifty Years Later."

32. "Integrate," Online Etymology Dictionary, accessed April 27, 2015, https://www.etymonline.com/.

33. "New Orleans civil rights pioneer Ruby Bridges to be honored with statue," *The Associated Press*, November 14, 2014, https://web.archive.org/web/20141117014209/https://www.nola.com/education/index.ssf/2014/11/ruby_bridges_new_orleans_statu.html.

The Trail of Rice

34. "T-shirt saying Go Home, Cook Rice," Deviantart, accessed November 1, 2014, https://web.archive.org/web/20240917110258/https://www.deviantart.com/xxguccixgirlxx/art/Go-Home-Cook-Rice-59655609; "go home cook rice! save money!," video, posted December 10, 2008, by Kai Dela Cruz, YouTube, https://www.youtube.com/watch?v=_x7viRnyTrs; "Mug: go home cook rice," Zazzle, accessed November 1, 2014, https://www.zazzle.ca/go_home_cook_rice_mug+168347217380219873 (page discontinued); Joan Namkoong, *Go Home, Cook Rice: A Guide to Buying and Cooking the Fresh Foods of Hawaii* (Namkoong Publishing, 2001).
35. "What is Rice?," Rice, Simply Rice, accessed November 1, 2014, https://web.archive.org/web/20190905191812/http://www.philrice.net/what-is-rice/.
36. "What is Rice?," Rice, Simply Rice.
37. "Home of the—Capitals of the World," Arkansas Department of Parks & Tourism, accessed November 1, 2014, https://web.archive.org/web/20090415215536/http://www.arkansas.com/uniquely%2Darkansas/capitals/. The title is also claimed by Stuttgart.
38. Judith A. Carney, "From Hands to Tutors: African Expertise in South Carolina Rice Economy," *Agricultural History*, Summer (1993): 11–13, 38.
39. Judith A. Carney, *Black Rice: The African Origins of Rice Cultivation in the Americas* (Harvard University Press, 2002), 91.
40. *Evening Gazette*, July 11, 1785, quoted in Robert M. Weir, Karen Hess, *The Carolina Rice Kitchen: The African Connection* (University of South Carolina Press, 1998), 13; Louis D. DeSaussure, "55 Prime Negroes, Accustomed to the Culture of Rice, 1857," still image, Emergence of Advertising in America: 1850–1920, https://idn.duke.edu/ark:/87924/r44m9318g; J. S. Ryan, "List of Negroes For Sale By J. S, Ryan At Public Auction," 1857, still image, Emergence of Advertising in America: 1850–1920, https://idn.duke.edu/ark:/87924/r4w66c001; Warren Lee Goss, "Fictional advertisement, an illustration from 'Tom Clifton....' by Warren Lee Goss, 1892: 'Gang of 25 Sea Island Cotton and Rice Negroes,'" 1892, still image, Broadus R. Littlejohn Jr. Manuscript and Ephemera Collection, https://

digitalcommons.wofford.edu/littlejohnmss/323; the website Vintage Ad Browser (site discontinued) had image fliers of the time advertising sales of experienced African rice farmers.

41. "Charles Manigault's Gowrie—A Starting Point," SciWay, accessed November 1, 2014, https://www.sciway.net/afam/slavery/gowrie.html.

42. "Inflation Calculator," Dave Manual, accessed November 1, 2014, https://www.davemanuel.com/inflation-calculator.php.

43. Paul Sutter and Christopher J. Manganiello, eds., *Environmental History and the American South: A Reader* (University of Georgia, 2009), 94.

44. "Africans in the Low Country," National Park Service, accessed November 1, 2014, https://www.nps.gov/ethnography/aah/AAheritage/lowCountryA.htm.

45. James E. McWilliams, *A Revolution in Eating: How the Quest for Food Shaped America* (Columbia University, 2013), 156, EPUB.

46. US CONST. art. I. §10. §§2.

47. Paul Finkelman, "Garrison's Constitution the Covenant with Death and How it Was Made," *Prologue Magazine*, winter 2000, vol. 32, no. 4, https://www.archives.gov/publications/prologue/2000/winter/garrisons-constitution-1.

48. F. Hall, *The Importance of the British Plantations in America to this Kingdom* (London: Printed for J. Peele, 1731): https://archive.org/details/importanceofbrit00hall/page/12/mode/2up; Edward Eggleston, "One Little Bag of Rice," in *Stories of Great Americans for Little Americans* (American Book Company, 1985): https://archive.org/details/storiesofgreatam00eggl.

49. "Rice Fields and Sections 106," South Carolina Department of Archives and History/State Historic Preservation Office, 2011, https://scdah.sc.gov/sites/scdah/files/Documents/Images/Rice%20Fields%20and%20Section%20106.pdf.

50. Robert F. W. Allston, *The South Carolina Rice Plantation As Revealed in the Papers of Robert F. Allston* (University of South Carolina, 2004), Google Play Books.

51. "History of Rice," American Rice Inc., accessed November 1, 2014, https://web.archive.org/web/20040113024350/http://www.amrice.com/6-0.cfm; "Agriculture in South Carolina," South Carolina

Department of Agriculture, accessed November 1, 2014, https://agriculture.sc.gov/about/.

52. Judith A. Carney, "'With Grains in Her Hair': Rice in Colonial Brazil," *Slavery and Abolition*, vol. 25, no.1 (2004): 1-27, https://geog.ucla.edu/sites/default/files/users/carney/33.pdf.

53. Lerone Bennett Jr., "First Generation," (*Ebony Magazine*, 1995): 186, https://books.google.com/books?id=8_W-QMJlBHIC&lpg=PA1&pg=PA3#v=onepage&q&f=false.

54. Robert M. Weir and Karen Hess, *The Carolina Rice Kitchen: The African Connection* (University of South Carolina Press, 1998), 10.

55. "Agriculture in South Carolina," South Carolina Department of Agriculture, accessed November 1, 2014, https://agriculture.sc.gov/about/.

56. Carney, *Black Rice*, 32.

57. Carney, *Black Rice*, 12, 37.

58. Carney, *Black Rice*, 161.

59. "History of the South Carolina State Fair and History of Agriculture in South Carolina," South Carolina State Fair, archived June 19, 2014, https://web.archive.org/web/20140619083326/http://www.scstatefair.org/p/297.

60. American Rice Inc., "History of Rice."

61. "Colonial Economy," History.com, archived March 8, 2010, at https://web.archive.org/web/20100308071940/http://www.history.com/topics/colonial-economy.

62. Joseph Opala, "The Gullah: Rice, Slavery and the Sierra Leone-American Connection," Yale, archived November 4, 2014 at https://web.archive.org/web/20060504182125/http://yale.edu/glc/gullah/02.htm.

63. Untitled review of *Black Rice: The African Origins of Rice Cultivation in the Americas* by Judith A. Carney, *The Journal of Blacks in Higher Education*, no. 34 (2001): 131. https://doi.org/10.2307/3134146.

64. "The 'rice-and-beans' of Brazilian Food," Authentic Brazilian Cuisine, archived July 15, 2015, at https://web.archive.org/web/20141014121108/http://authenticbraziliancuisine.blogspot.com/2010/02/rice-and-beans-of-brazilian-food.html.

65. "New Orleans: Seven Brothers of the Blood," Esoteric Philosopher: Study of the Endless Path of Wisdom, archived April 04, 2016, at

https://web.archive.org/web/20160404061549/http://logos_endless_summer.tripod.com/id105.html.

66. "Glossary of Words, Phrases, Things & Persons," New Orleans Historic Voodoo Museum, archived September 13, 2014, at https://web.archive.org/web/20140913130242/http://www.voodoomuseum.com/index.php?option=com_content&view=article&id=36.

67. Jessica B. Harris, *High on the Hog: A Culinary Journey from Africa to America* (Bloomsbury Publishing, 2011), 76.

68. E. W. Warren, *Mrs. Hill's New Cook Book* (1872), quoted in Robert M. Weir and Karen Hess, *Carolina Rice Kitchen: The African Connection* (University of South Carolina Press, 1998), 30–31.

69. E. W. Warren, *Mrs. Hill's Cook Book*, 15.

70. E. W. Warren, *Mrs. Hill's Cook Book*, 10.

71. "Slavery on South Carolina Rice Plantations: The Migration of People and Knowledge in Early Colonial America," Rice Diversity, accessed June 11, 2015, http://www.ricediversity.org/outreach/educatorscorner/documents/Carolina-Gold-Student-handout.pdf.

72. Brandon Kelly, Jacob Barron, and Joel Barron, "Early Agriculture in Louisiana," chap. 8, EPUB, http://www.latech.edu/tech/liberal-arts/geography/courses/310/text/hist_ag.htm (page discontinued).

73. Marcus Christian, *The History of The Negro in Louisiana*, University of New Orleans Digital Collections, accessed November 1, 2014, http://louisdl.louislibraries.org/cgi-bin/showfile.exe?CISOROOT=/p15140coll42&CISOPTR=76&CISOMODE=print (site discontinued).

74. "Fact Sheet for Slavery in Early New Orleans and Louisiana," Sonoma State University, accessed November 20, 2014, http://www.sonoma.edu/tah2/lessons/jolly/mississippi/slavery_new_orleans_louisiana.rtf (site discontinued).

75. Peter H. Wood, *Black Majority: Negros in Colonial South Carolina from 1670 through the Stono Rebellion*, (New York: Alfred A. Knopf, 1975); Daniel Littlefield, *Ethnicity and Slave Trade in Colonial South Carolina* (University of Illinois Press, 1991).

76. Edda L. Fields-Black, *Deep Roots: Rice Farmers in West Africa and the African Diaspora* (Indiana University Press, 2014).

77. Orlando Ribeiro, *Aspectos y Problemas De Expansao Portuguesa* (Foundation of Casa de Bragança, 1955), quoted in Judith A. Carney,

Black Rice: The African Origins of Rice Cultivation in the Americas (Harvard University Press, 2001), 142.
78. Judith Carney, *Black Rice*, 163.
79. Joseph E. Halloway.
80. Robert F. W. Allston, et al.

A Peck of Dirt

81. C. Ray Brassieur, "Feeling Like Choupique on the Blacktop? Rx: Daily Doses of Folk Culture in Context," Folklife in Louisiana, archived October 21, 2014, at https://web.archive.org/web/20141021030357/http://www.louisianafolklife.org/LT/Articles_Essays/lfmchoupique.html.
82. "Myths and Regulations," Bowfin Anglers' Group, archived August 16, 2014, at https://web.archive.org/web/20140816021254/http://bowfinanglers.com/myths.html.
83. Lexi Krock, "Other Fish in the Sea," NOVA, December 31, 2002, https://www.pbs.org/wgbh/nova/article/other-fish-sea/.
84. C. Ray Brassieur, "Feeling Like Choupique?"
85. "Jurassic Crawfish Fossil Found," *The Japan Times*, July 18, 2010, http://www.japantimes.co.jp/news/2010/07/18/national/jurassic-crawfish-fossil- found/#.U3RI7cavvlI (page discontinued).
86. "Bogolan: The Art of Making Mudcloth," African Heritage, September 11, 2009, archived September 17, 2014, at https://web.archive.org/web/20140917222207/http://afrolegends.com/2009/09/11/bogolan-the-art-of-making-mudcloth/.
87. Hilda Hertz, "Notes on Clay and Starch Eating Among Negroes in a Southern Urban Community," *Social Forces*, 25, no. 3 (1947): 343, https://doi.org/10.1093/SF/25.3.343.
88. William E. Schmidt, "Southern Practice of Eating Dirt Shows Signs of Waning," *The New York Times*, February 13, 1984, https://www.nytimes.com/1984/02/13/us/southern-practice-of-eating-dirt-shows-signs-of-waning.html.

89. Kevin L. Callahan, "Pica, Geophagy, and Rock-Art in the Eastern United States," in *The Rock-Art of Eastern North America: Capturing Images and Insight*, ed. Carol Diaz-Granados and James R. Duncan (University of Alabama Press, 2004), 73.
90. Robert W. Twyman, "The Clay Eater: A New Look at an Old Southern Enigma," *The Journal of Southern History*, 37, no. 3 (1971): 439–448, https://doi.org/10.2307/2206950.
91. Callahan, "Pica, Geophagy, and Rock-Art," 71–73.
92. *Oxford English Dictionary* (Online, 2014), under "Cachexia."
93. Twyman, "The Clay Eater," 446.
94. Beth Ann Fennelly, "Beth Ann Fennelly Digs into Geophagy," *Oxford American*, no. 68, March 9, 2010, http://www.oxfordamerican.org/articles/2010/mar/09/wide-%20world-eating-dirt/ (page discontinued).
95. Twyman, "The Clay Eater," 440.
96. Fennelly, "Beth Ann Fennelly Digs into Geophagy."
97. Callahan, "Pica, Geophagy, and Rock-Art," 68.
98. Callahan, "Pica, Geophagy, and Rock-Art," 68.
99. "Words From the Crone," Revrita, July 29, 2012, http://revrita.com/crone/2012/07/a-peck-of-dirt/ (site discontinued).
100. Katie Fox, "Let Your Kids get Dirty!," The Art of Simple, June 25, 2010, https://www.theartofsimple.net/let-your-kids-get-dirty/.
101. Sarah Gilbert, "Has Your Child Had His Peck of Dirt Today?," Parent Dish, October 1, 2004, http://www.parentdish.com/2004/10/01/has-your-child-had-his-peck-of- dirt-today/ (site discontinued).
102. Chris Lowry, "Bacteria Found in the Soil Activated a Group of Neurons that Produce the Brain Chemical Serotonin," Medical News Today, April 4, 2007, http://www.medicalnewstoday.com/releases/66838.php.
103. Anne Zimmerman, "Tasting Dirt: The Continuity of Terroir, First-Hand," Culinate, September 21, 2009, http://www.culinate.com/search/q,vt=top,q=dirt/235913 (site discontinued).
104. Laura Parker, "Tasting Notes," Taste of Place, archived May 8, 2015, at https://web.archive.org/web/20150508074819/http://www.lauraparkerstudio.com/tasteofplace/tastingnotes.html.
105. *Dictionary.com*, under synesthesia.
106. *Urban Dictionary*, under Smaste.

107. Twyman, "The Clay Eater," 446–48.

108. "Eating Dirt: It Might Be Good for You," ABC News, updated October 3, 2005, http://abcnews.go.com/Health/Diet/story?id=1167623&page=1&singlePage=true.

109. Twyman, "The Clay Eater," 446.

110. Schmidt, "Southern Practice of Eating Dirt."

111. Deborah Mason, "Blackened Red Dirt and Other Delicacies," *The New York Times*, April 2, 1989, http://www.nytimes.com/1989/04/02/books/blackened-red-dirt-and-other-delicacies.html.

112. Schmidt, "Southern Practice of Eating Dirt."

113. Kurt Schlosser, "Shailene Woodley Gives Letterman the Dirt on Eating Clay," Today, May 6, 2014, https://www.today.com/entertainment/shailene-woodley-gives-letterman-dirt-eating-clay-2D79628004.

114. Jennifer Gauntt, "Professor Digs Into Geophagy Research," Sam Houston State University News, archived September 15, 2014, at https://web.archive.org/web/20140915212640/http://www.shsu.edu/~pin_www/T%40S/2010/geophagy.html.

115. "Clay May be Best Cure for Infections," Mississippi Miracle Clay, January 30, 2014, archived February 19, 2015, at https://web.archive.org/web/20150219094820/http://www.mississippimiracleclay.com/clay-may-be-best-cure-for-infections/.

116. Samuel M. Flaxman and Paul W. Sherman, "Morning Sickness: A Mechanism for Protecting Mother and Embryo," *The Quarterly Review of Biology*, 75, no. 2 (2000): 113–48, https://www.jstor.org/stable/2664252.

117. ABC News, "Eating Dirt: It Might Be Good For You."

118. Callahan, "Pica, Geophagy, and Rock-Art," 71.

119. Z. H. McMahan and H. L. Dupont, "The History of Acute Infectious Diarrhoea management—From Poorly Focused Empiricism to Fluid Therapy and Modern Pharmacotherapy," *Alimentary Pharmacology & Therapeutics*, 25, no. 7 (2007): 759–69, https://doi.org/10.1111/j.1365-2036.2007.03261.x.

120. Paul A. Schroeder, "Kaolin," New Georgia Encyclopedia, updated July 31, 2018, https://www.georgiaencyclopedia.org/articles/business-economy/kaolin.

121. Chuck Reece, "Making Peace with the Age-Old Practice of Eating White Dirt," accessed November 4, 2014, https://bittersoutherner.com/eat-white-dirt/#.U4BVRsavtFI.
122. Jamil S. Zainaldin, "Great Depression," New Georgia Encyclopedia, updated September 29, 2020, https://www.georgiaencyclopedia.org/articles/history-archaeology/great-depression.
123. Reece, "Making Peace."
124. "We Provide Wonderful White Dirt for Individuals who Love White Clay. Give it a Try," Georgia White Dirt, archived June 30, 2013 at https://web.archive.org/web/20130630083503/http://www.georgiawhitedirt.com:80/; "The Original Georgia Grown Gourmet White Dirt," White Dirt of Georgia, archived February 10, 2009, at https://web.archive.org/web/20090210205447/http://whitedirt.samsbiz.com:80/; "Using Bentonite, Illite & Montmorrilonite Healing Clays Internally," Eyton's Earth, archived July 23, 2005, at https://web.archive.org/web/20050723023709/http://www.eytonsearth.org/drinking-clay-internal-use.php; "Welcome to Australian Healing Clay," Australian Healing Clay, archived May 23, 2013, at https://web.archive.org/web/20130523121514/http://healingclay.com.au/; "From the Depths of the Earth . . . Truly a Miracle of Healing," Mississippi Miracle Clay, archived August 6, 2014, at https://web.archive.org/web/20140806124005/http://mississippimiracleclay.com/; "Edible Clay, Can it Really be Good for you?," Clay Remedies, archived April 2, 2016, at https://web.archive.org/web/20160402021034/http://www.clayremedies.com/; "Contact Us," Home Grown Georgia White Dirt, archived January 6, 2014, at https://web.archive.org/web/20140106190819/https://whitedirtga.com/contactus.sc; "Fuller's Earth Clay," Mountain Rose Herbs, archived April 1, 2021, at https://web.archive.org/web/20210401152826/https://mountainroseherbs.com/fullers-earth-clay.

Dueling With Martin

125. "André Cailloux, Civil War Hero," African American Registry, http://www.aaregistry.org/historic_events/view/Andre-cailloux-civil-war-hero (page discontinued).

126. Donald R. Shaffer, "Free Soldiers of Color," *The New York Times*, February 17, 2012, https://archive.nytimes.com/opinionator.blogs.nytimes.com/2012/02/17/free-soldiers-of-color/.
127. Shaffer, "Free Soldiers of Color."
128. Shaffer, "Free Soldiers of Color."
129. Jerome S. Handler and Michael L. Tuite Jr., "Retouching History: The Modern Falsification of a Civil War Photograph," The University of Virginia, August 20, 2009, archived November 21, 2016, at https://web.archive.org/web/20161121132842/http://jeromehandler.org/wp-content/uploads/Retouching-History-05.pdf.
130. Marc Wortman, "True Colors," *Smithsonian Magazine*, October 2014, 70.
131. Donald R. Shaffer, "Benjamin Butler Betrays Louisiana Slaves, Part 2," Civil War Emancipation, August 2, 2012, https://cwemancipation.wordpress.com/2012/08/02/benjamin-butler-betrays-louisiana-slaves-part-2/.
132. "Just Learning To Be Men," in *These Men Will Be Good Soldiers* (US Colored Troops Formed in North Carolina, 1999), https://www.ncgenweb.us/hyde/military/ncusct/shana1.htm.
133. "Just Learning To Be Men."
134. John David Winters, *The Civil War in Louisiana* (LSU Press, 1991), 207, Google Play Books.
135. Winters, *The Civil War*, 208.
136. Patricia L. Faust quoted in *The Southern Journey of a Civil War Marine: The Illustrated Note-Book of Henry O. Gusley*, Edward T. Cotham Jr. (University of Texas Press, 2009), 188, Google Play Books.
137. Shaffer, "Benjamin Butler Betrays Louisiana Slaves."
138. "USCT In The South and The First Black Soldiers," accessed November 29, 2014 (site discontinued).
139. "Search for Soldiers," National Park Service, https://www.nps.gov/civilwar/search-soldiers.htm; "Guillory, Martin," National Park Service, https://www.nps.gov/civilwar/search-soldiers-detail.htm?soldierId=EE28B6A3-DC7A-DF11-BF36-B8AC6F5D926A; "Cailloux, Andre," National Park Service, https://www.nps.gov/civilwar/search-soldiers-detail.htm?soldierId=89502F8A-DC7A-DF11-BF36-B8AC6F5D926A; "Cailloux, Andre," National Park Services, https://www.nps.gov/civilwar/search-

soldiers-detail.htm?soldierId=8A502F8A-DC7A-DF11-BF36-B8AC6F5D926A.

140. C. P. Weaver, *Thank God My regiment an African One: The Civil War Diary of Colonel Nathan W. Daniels* (LSU Press, 2000), 158.

141. Leah Binkovitz, "The Uncertain Promise of Freedom's Light: Black Soldiers in the Civil War," *Smithsonian Museum*, February 1, 2013, https://www.smithsonianmag.com/smithsonian-institution/the-uncertain-promise-of-freedoms-light-black-soldiers-in-the-civil-war-9660675/.

142. "Louisiana Native Guards on Ship Island 1863–1870," National Park Services, archived October 13, 2006, at https://web.archive.org/web/20061013025000/http://www.nps.gov/archive/guis/extended/MIS/MHistory/NatvGrd.htm.

143. Jim Hollandsworth, *The Louisiana Native Guards: The Black Military Experience During the Civil War* (LSU Press, 1998).

144. Joelle Jackson, "USA / Corps d'Afrique 1st Louisiana Native Guard (1862–1863)," BlackPast, June 23, 2011, https://www.blackpast.org/african-american-history/1st-louisiana-native-guard-usa-corps-d-afrique-1862-1863/.

145. William F. Fox, *The Colored Troops: Fox's Regimental Losses*, Chapter 6, archived April 10, 2015, at https://web.archive.org/web/20150410161819/http://www.civilwarhome.com/chapt6.htm.

146. "Union Soldiers at Port Hudson," The Hardy Party, accessed December 11, 2014, https://pth.thehardyparty.com/fed_soldiers.htm.

147. "USCT in the South."

148. E. Longpie, quoted in *Black and American Indian Soldiers in the Civil War*, Joseph T. Wilson and Annie Heloise Abel (AfterMath, 2013).

149. "USCT in the South."

150. "Andre Cailloux, Businessman, and Soldier Born," African American Registry, accessed November 29, 2014, https://aaregistry.org/story/andre-cailloux-civil-war-hero/.

151. "USCT in the South."

152. Natasha Trethewey, *Native Guard* (Houghton Mifflin, 2007), 48.

153. "USCT in the South."

154. Steven Mintz, ed., *African American Voices: A Documentary Reader, 1619–1877* (Wiley-Blackwell, 2009), EPUB.

155. "USCT in the South."
156. African American Registry, "Andre Cailloux."
157. "Military Research Forum," AfriGeneas, accessed November 29, 2014, http://www.afrigeneas.com/forum-militaryarchive/index.cgi/md/read/id/339/sbj/reference-port- hudson-la-massacre/ (site discontinued).
158. William Wells Brown, *The Negro in the American Rebellion: His Heroism and His Fidelity* (Lee & Shepard, 1867), 176.
159. Joseph Thomas Wilson, *The Black Phalanx: African American Soldiers in the War of Independence, the War of 1812, and the Civil War* (Da Capo Press, 1994), 396.
160. "Port Hudson," National Park Service, archived August 19, 2010, at https://web.archive.org/web/20100819180737/http://www.nps.gov/nr/travel/louisiana/por.htm; "Union Soldiers at Port Hudson," The Hardy Party. Overall losses among all Union soldiers was estimated at 496 killed, 2,945 wounded, and 358 missing.
161. Brown, *The Negro in the American Rebellion*, 173.
162. "Port Hudson State Historic Site," Louisiana State Park Historic Sites, archived April 6, 2014, at https://web.archive.org/web/20140406004255/http://www.crt.state.la.us/louisiana-state-parks/historic-sites/port-hudson-state-historic-site/index.
163. Longpie, in *Black and American Indian Soldiers.*
164. Brown, *The Negro in the American Rebellion*, 173.
165. Longpie, in *Black and American Indian Soldiers.*
166. Brown, *The Negro in the American Rebellion*, 172.
167. Longpie, in *Black and American Indian Soldiers.*
168. Brown, *The Negro in the American Rebellion*, 176.
169. "Proclamation by the Confederate President," Freedmen and Southern Society Project, updated February 2, 2025, https://www.freedmen.umd.edu/pow.htm.
170. Celine Fremaux Garcia, "Celine: Remembering Louisiana, 1850–1871," quoted in *The Louisiana Native Guards*, Jim Hollandsworth, http://files.usgwarchives.net/la/state/military/afriamer/natguard.txt.
171. "Genealogy and History Forum Archive 3," AfriGeneas, http://www.afrigeneas.com/forum-aarchive/index_3.cgi/md/read/id/23398 (site discontinued).
172. Trethewey, *Native Guard*, 40–49.

173. "Fort Pillow Massacre," History.com, accessed November 29, 2014, http://www.history.com/topics/american-civil-war/fort-pillow-massacre.
174. National Park Service, "Louisiana Native Guards."
175. Trethewey, *Native Guard*, 48; National Park Service, "Louisiana Native Guards."
176. "From George Washington to Bryan Fairfax, 24 August 1774," Founders Online, https://founders.archives.gov/GEWN-02-10-02-0097.
177. Glen Ford, "A Monument to George Washington's Slaves," The Black Commentator, June 27, 2002, https://blackcommentator.com/washingtons_slaves.html.
178. Mary Miley Theobald, "The Monstrous Absurdity: The Gunpowder Theft Examined," *CW Journal* (2006), archived June 19, 2015, at https://web.archive.org/web/20150619184523/http://www.history.org/foundation/journal/summer06/plots.cfm.
179. Thomas Jefferson et al., "The Declaration of Independence," accessed December 3, 2014, http://www.archives.gov/exhibits/charters/declaration_transcript.html. The entire passage includes a similar denunciation of British attempts to gain support from Native Americans: "He has excited domestic insurrections amongst us, and has endeavoured to bring on the inhabitants of our frontiers, the merciless Indian Savages, whose known rule of warfare, is an undistinguished destruction of all ages, sexes and conditions."
180. Erica Armstrong Dunbar, "George Washington, Slave Catcher," *The New York Times*, February 16, 2015, https://www.nytimes.com/2015/02/16/opinion/george-washington-slave-catcher.html?referrer&_r=0.
181. "George and Harry Washington Fight for Freedom," History? Because It's Here, https://historybecauseitshere.weebly.com/george-and-harry-washington-fight-for-freedom.html.
182. "Washington's Runaway Slaves," Black Loyalist, archived September 12, 2015, at https://web.archive.org/web/20150912054753/http://www.blackloyalist.info/washington-s-runaway-slaves.
183. "Treaty of Paris," Black Loyalist, accessed December 3, 2014, http://www.blackloyalist.info/treaty-of-paris/ (site discontinued).

184. "Washington's Revolution (Harry that is, not George)," Black Loyalist, archived February 11, 2012, at https://web.archive.org/web/20120211003300/http://www.blackloyalist.info/washington-s-revolution-harry-that-is-not-george/.
185. Black Loyalist, "Treaty of Paris."
186. "Bunce Island Exhibit," Kennesaw State University, archived August 22, 2015, at https://web.archive.org/web/20150822060634/http://www.kennesaw.edu/bunceisland/.
187. "Milestone Documents," National Archives, updated August 3, 2022, https://www.archives.gov/milestone-documents/list.
188. History? Because It's Here, "George and Harry Washington."
189. Eschool, "Chapter 6: The Revolution Within," 242, http://eschool2.bsd7.org/pluginfile.php/36160/mod_resource/content/1/Chapter_6.pdf (site discontinued).
190. Black Loyalist, "Washington's Revolution."
191. Boston King, "Memoirs of the Life of Boston King, a Black Preacher," *The Methodist Magazine* (March 1798): 106–10, 21, History Matters, http://historymatters.gmu.edu/d/6615/.
192. Boston King, "Memoirs of the Life of Boston King."
193. Black Loyalist, "Washington's Revolution."
194. Sylvia R. Frey, 192–93.
195. Black Loyalist, "Evacuation of New York," archived May 2, 2015, at https://web.archive.org/web/20150502141721/http://www.blackloyalist.info/evacuation-of-new-york/.
196. Sylvia R. Frey, 193.
197. Black Loyalist, "Evacuation of New York."
198. Sylvia R. Frey, 192–93.
199. Sylvia R. Frey, 193.
200. Black Loyalist, "Evacuation of New York."
201. Black Loyalist, "Washington's Revolution."
202. Black Loyalist, "Washington's Revolution."
203. Eliga H. Gould, "How Did the British Press Cover the American Revolution? And What Lessons Does this History Hold for Today's Upheavals?," *Foreign Policy*, July 3, 2012, https://foreignpolicy.com/2012/07/03/how-did-the-british-press-cover-the-american-revolution/.
204. Sylvia R. Frey, 174.

205. Timothy J. Lockley, "Slavery in Revolutionary Georgia," updated September 29, 2020, https://www.georgiaencyclopedia.org/articles/history-archaeology/slavery-in-revolutionary-georgia/.
206. Sylvia R. Frey, 175.
207. Sylvia R. Frey, 177.
208. Jill Lepore, "Goodbye, Columbus," *The New Yorker*, May 8, 2006, https://www.newyorker.com/magazine/2006/05/08/goodbye-columbus?printable=true&ixzz2ZBeO6EwR.
209. Sylvia R. Frey, 186.
210. Sylvia R. Frey, 177.
211. History? Because It's Here, "George and Harry Washington"; Black Loyalist, "Evacuation of New York."
212. Sylvia R. Frey, 193–94.
213. "Harry Washington," Black Loyalist, archived July 7, 2015, at https://web.archive.org/web/20150707221906/http://www.blackloyalist.info/person/display/1485.
214. Sylvia R. Frey, 197.
215. Sylvia R. Frey, 195–96.
216. Black Loyalist, "Washington's Revolution."
217. Sylvia R. Frey, 197.
218. Kathy Warnes, "Freedom Fighters George and Harry Washington," Searching Historical Horizon, archived January 29, 2013, at https://web.archive.org/web/20130129071355/http://searchinghistoricalhorizons.wordpress.com/2013/01/26/freedom-fighters-george-and-harry-washington/.
219. Black Loyalist, "Washington's Revolution."
220. Black Loyalist, "Washington's Revolution."
221. Black Loyalist, "Washington's Revolution."
222. "The Peace Treaties Signed at Paris and Versailles on 3 September 1783," Xenophon Group, archived April 25, 2015, at https://web.archive.org/web/20150424181401/http://xenophongroup.com/mcjoynt/1783_Treaties.htm; "The Father of Our Country," Geocaching, archived September 17, 2024, at https://web.archive.org/web/20240917005936/http://www.geocaching.com/geocache/GC3AYMN_henry-laurens?guid=4dbd0e4b-9eda-43dc-9b99-c54d06e7414b.

223. "History Essays: Treaty of Paris," The Lehrman Institute, https://lehrmaninstitute.org/history/treaty-of-paris.html; Edward Renehan, *The Treaty of Paris: the Precursor to a New Nation* (Infobase Publishing, 2009), EPUB.
224. The Lehrman Institute, "History Essays."
225. The Lehrman Institute, "History Essays."
226. Jake Sudderth, "Jay and Slavery," Columbia University Libraries, accessed December 4, 2014, https://dlc.library.columbia.edu/jay/jayandslavery.
227. The Lehrman Institute, "History Essays."
228. The Lehrman Institute, "History Essays."
229. Hugh Thomas, *The Slave Trade: The Story of the Atlantic Slave Trade 1440–1870* (Simon and Schuster, 2013), 486.
230. "Unveiling of New Treaty of Paris Painting by David Wagner," Maryland Society Sons of the American Revelation, archived October 28, 2010, at https://web.archive.org/web/20101028204121/http://www.marylandsar.org/News/Treaty-of-Paris-Painting-unveiling.
231. Dunbar, "George Washington, Slave Catcher."
232. Dunbar, "George Washington, Slave Catcher."
233. Sylvia R. Frey, 201.
234. Gould, "How Did the British Press Cover the American Revolution?"

Everyday Ekphrasis

235. Ben Radford, "Art, Mysteries and Context," *Skeptical Inquirer*, 36, no. 5 (2012): https://skepticalinquirer.org/2012/09/art-mysteries-and-context/.
236. Lianna Patch, "Massive, 'Lifelike' Show Blurs Lines of Reality at NOMA," NOLA Defender, archived March 21, 2013, at https://web.archive.org/web/20130321174105/http://www.noladefender.com/content/ba45nal-bl2iss.
237. Doug MacCash, "'Lifelike' At The New Orleans Museum of Art is a Mind-blowing New Show," NOLA.com, archived November 14, 2012, at https://web.archive.org/web/20121114092122/http://www.nola.com/arts/index.ssf/2012/11/lifelike_the_new_orleans_museu.html.

238. Robert Gober, *Newspaper*, 1992, photolithograph on paper, twine, 4.25 × 15.75 × 14 inches, Walker Art Center, Minneapolis, archived December 30, 2015, at https://web.archive.org/web/20151230005553/http://www.walkerart.org/collections/artworks/newspaper.
239. Siri Engberg et al., "Lifelike," Artbook, archived October 13, 2012, at https://web.archive.org/web/20121013155837/http://www.artbook.com/9780935640687.html.
240. "Daniel Douke," Artnet.com, archived November 18, 2014, at https://www.artnet.com/artists/daniel-douke/.
241. MacCash, "'Lifelike.'"
242. Joey Franklin, "Essayings 'The Thing': An Imagiste Approach to the Lyric Essay," The Haiku Foundation, September 2012, accessed May 29, 2025, https://www.thehaikufoundation.org/omeka/files/original/5da749c8c1f41dff85d8dcfa8e0a502c.pdf.

About the Author

Brenda D. Quant was born in New Orleans, Louisiana. She obtained her bachelor's degree in English from the University of New Orleans in 1968. She enrolled in the UNO Creative Writing Low-Residency Program in 2004 and the UNO Creative Writing Workshop in 2010, receiving her MFA in creative writing in 2015.

In 2013, Quant was awarded the Malcolm Magaw Prize for Best Graduate Student Essay, the Samuel Mockbee Nonfiction Award, and the Gulf Coast Association of Creative Writing Teachers Graduate Award for Nonfiction. Quant received a Literature Fellowship from the Louisiana State Division of the Arts in 1991. Her work appeared in *Fjords Review, The New Orleans Tribune, The Other Side, African American Review, Thema Literary Quarterly,* and other publications. She died in 2022.